Advanced Studies
Mobile Research Center Bremen

Edited by
O. Herzog,
C. Görg,
M. Lawo,
Bremen, Germany

T0238481

Das Mobile Research Center Bremen (MRC) im Technologie-Zentrum Informatik und Informationstechnik (TZI) der Universität Bremen erforscht, entwickelt und erprobt in enger Zusammenarbeit mit der Wirtschaft mobile Informatik-, Informations- und Kommunikationstechnologien. Als Forschungs- und Transferinstitut des Landes Bremen vernetzt und koordiniert das MRC hochschulübergreifend eine Vielzahl von interdisziplinären Arbeitsgruppen, die sich mit der Entwicklung und Anwendung mobiler Lösungen beschäftigen. Die Reihe „Advanced Studies" präsentiert ausgewählte hervorragende Arbeitsergebnisse aus der Forschungstätigkeit der Mitglieder des MRC.

In close collaboration with the industry, the Mobile Research Center Bremen (MRC), a division of the Center for Computing and Communication Technologies (TZI) of the University of Bremen, investigates, develops and tests mobile computing, information and communication technologies. This research cluster of the state of Bremen links and coordinates interdisciplinary research teams from different universities and institutions, which are concerned with the development and application of mobile solutions. The series "Advanced Studies" presents a selection of outstanding results of MRC's research projects.

Edited by
Prof. Dr. Otthein Herzog
Prof. Dr. Carmelita Görg
Prof. Dr. Michael Lawo
Mobile Research Center, Bremen, Germany

Yasir Zaki

Future Mobile Communications

LTE Optimization and Mobile Network Virtualization

 Springer Vieweg

RESEARCH

Yasir Zaki
Bremen, Germany

Dissertation University of Bremen, 2012

Printed with friendly support of
MRC Mobile Research Center, University of Bremen

ISBN 978-3-658-00807-9   ISBN 978-3-658-00808-6 (eBook)
DOI 10.1007/978-3-658-00808-6

The Deutsche Nationalbibliothek lists this publication in the Deutsche Nationalbibliografie; detailed bibliographic data are available in the Internet at http://dnb.d-nb.de.

Library of Congress Control Number: 2012953090

Springer Vieweg
© Springer Fachmedien Wiesbaden 2013

Printed on acid-free paper

Springer Vieweg is a brand of Springer DE.
Springer DE is part of Springer Science+Business Media.
www.springer-vieweg.de

To my beloved wife Tamara Hamed and to my parents.

Acknowledgments

It would not have been possible to finish this work and write the thesis without the help and support of all the kind people around me, to only some of whom it is possible to give particular mention here. I would like to thank my beloved wife Tamara Hamed, for her unconditional support and great patience. I will forever owe her a debt of gratitude for always believing in me, even in the times when I didn't. I would also like to thank my parents, who have given me their un-equivalent support, for which my mere expression of thanks likewise does not suffice. And to my life joy, my kids, Tanya and Yezin.

This thesis would not have seen the light without the help and support of my supervisor, Prof. Dr. Carmelita Görg. Her wide knowledge, encouragement and personal guidance have been of great value to me. I would also like to express my gratitude to Prof. Dr.-Ing. Andreas Timm-Giel, for all his valuable input.

The good advice, support and friendship of my colleague, Dr. Thushara Weerawardane has been invaluable on both academic and personal level, for which I am extremely grateful. During this work I have collaborated with many colleagues for whom I have great respect, in particular I wish to extend my warmest thanks to Dr. Koojana Kuladinithi and Asanga Udugama for their professional and personal support. I would also like to express my gratitude to Dr. Hadeer Hamed and Mr. Khalis Mahmoud Khalis for their efforts in revising the thesis.

I would like to acknowledge all of my friends and colleagues within the ComNets department of the University of Bremen. Dr. Xi Li for her help in proof reading the thesis, Liang Zhao for being a great colleague in all the projects we worked together. Lots of gratitude to Dr. Andreas Könsgen, Markus Becker, Umar Toseef, Muhammed Mutakin Siddique, Aman Singh, Dr. Bernd-Ludwig Wenning, Martina Kamman and Karl-Heinz Volk for their support. In addition, I would also like to thank my students Nikola Zahariev and Safdar Nawaz Khan Marwat for their support and good work.

Finally, a special acknowledgment for the DAAD (German Academic Exchange Service), for giving me the chance to come to Germany to do my Master studies, which led eventually to the finishing of this doctoral thesis.

Yasir Zaki

Abstract

Providing QoS while optimizing the LTE network in a cost efficient manner is very challenging. Thus, radio scheduling is one of the most important functions in mobile broadband networks. The design of a mobile network radio scheduler holds several objectives that need to be satisfied, for example: the scheduler needs to maximize the radio performance by efficiently distributing the limited radio resources, since the operator's revenue depends on it. In addition, the scheduler has to guarantee the user's demands in terms of their Quality of Service (QoS). Thus, the design of an effective scheduler is rather a complex task. In this thesis, the author proposes the design of a radio scheduler that is optimized towards QoS guarantees and system performance optimization. The proposed scheduler is called "Optimized Service Aware Scheduler" (OSA). The OSA scheduler is tested and analyzed in several scenarios, and is compared against other known schedulers.

A novel wireless network virtualization framework is also proposed in this thesis. The framework targets the concepts of wireless virtualization applied within the 3GPP Long Term Evolution (LTE) system. LTE represents one of the new mobile communication systems that is just entering the market. Therefore, LTE was chosen as a case study to demonstrate the proposed wireless virtualization framework. The framework is implemented in the LTE network simulator and analyzed, highlighting the many advantages and potential gain that the virtualization process can achieve. Two potential gain scenarios that can result from using network virtualization in LTE systems are analyzed: Multiplexing gain coming from spectrum sharing, and multi-user diversity gain.

Several LTE radio analytical models, based on Continuous Time Markov Chains are designed and developed in this thesis. These models target the modeling of three different time domain radio schedulers: Maximum Throughput (MaxT), Blind Equal Throughput (BET), and Optimized Service Aware Scheduler (OSA). The models are used to obtain faster results (i.e., in a very short time period in the order of seconds to minutes), compared to the simulation results that can take considerably longer periods, such as hours or sometimes even days. The model results are also compared against the simulation results, and it is shown that it provides a good match. Thus, it can be used for fast radio dimensioning purposes.

Overall, the concepts, investigations, and the analytical models presented in this thesis can help mobile network operators to optimize their radio network and provide the necessary means to support services QoS differentiations and guarantees. In addition, the network virtualization concepts provides an excellent tool that can enable the operators to share their resources and reduce their cost, as well as provide good chances for smaller operators to enter the market.

Contents

List of Figures

List of Tables

List of Abbreviations

3GPP	3rd Generation Partnership Project	DSCP	Differentiated Services Code Point
AMC	Adaptive Modulation and Coding	DVB	Digital Video Broadcasting
		eNodeB	enhanced NodeB
AODV	Ad-hoc On-demand Distance Vector	E-UTRAN	Evolved Universal Terrestrial Radio Access Network
ARP	Allocation and Retention Priority	EDGE	Enhanced Data for GSM Evolution
ARQ	Automatic Repeat Request	EESM	Exponential Effective SINR Mapping
AUC	Authentication Center		
AWGN	Additive White Gaussian Noise	EFR	Enhanced Full Rate
		EMA	Exponential Moving Average
BET	Blind Equal Throughput	EPC	Evolved Packet Core
BLER	Block Error Rate	EPS	Evolved Packet System
BSC	Base Station Controller	FDD	Frequency Division Duplex
BSS	Base Station Subsystem	FDM	Frequency Domain Multiplexing
BTS	Base Transceiver Station		
CA	Carrier Aggregation	FDMA	Frequency Division Multiple Access
CDMA	Code Division Multiple Access	FDS	Frequency Domain Scheduler
		FTP	File Transfer Protocol
CN	Core Network	GBR	Guaranteed Bit Rate
CoMP	Coordinated Multi-Point	GMSK	Gaussian Minimum Shift Keying
CQI	Channel Quality Indicator		
CTMC	Continuous Time Markov Chain	GPRS	General Packet Radio Service
		GSM	Global System for Mobile Communication
DeNB	Donor eNodeB		
DL	Downlink	GTP	Gateway Tunneling Protocol

HARQ	Hybrid Automatic Repeat Request	PCRF	Policy and Charging Rules Function
HLR	Home Location Registry	PDA	Personal Digital Assistant
HSDPA	High Speed Downlink Packet Access	PDCP	Packet Data Convergence Protocol
HSPA	High Speed Packet Access	PDN	Packet Data Network
HSS	Home Subscriber Server	PDN-GW	Packet Data Network Gateway
HSUPA	High Speed Uplink Packet Access	PDU	Protocol Data Unit
		PHY	Physical Layer
HTTP	Hypertext Transfer Protocol	PRB	Physical Resource Block
IMU	International Mobile Telecommunication	PRBs	Physical Resource Blocks
		PSK	Phase Shift Keying
IP	Internet Protocol	PSTN	Public Switched Telephone Network
ISP	Internet Service Provider		
IT	Information Technology	QCI	QoS Class Identifier
ITU	International Telecommunication Union	QoS	Quality of Service
		RD	Random Direction
LTE	Long Term Evolution	RLC	Radio Link Control
MAC	Medium Access Channel	RN	Relay Node
MaxT	Maximum Throughput	RNC	Radio Network Controller
MCS	Modulation and Coding Scheme	RRC	Radio Resource Control
		RWP	Random Way Point
MIESM	Mutual Information Effective SINR Mapping	S-GW	Serving Gateway
		SAE	System Architecture Evolution
MIMO	Multi Input Multi Output	SAN	Storage Area Network
MME	Mobility Management Entity	SC-FDMA	Single Carrier Frequency Domain Multiple Access
MOS	Mean Opinion Score		
MS	Mobile Station	SDMA	Space Division Multiple Access
MSC	Mobile Switching Center		
non-GBR	non-Guaranteed Bit Rate	SDR	Software Defined Radio
OFDMA	Orthogonal Frequency Domain Multiple Access	SIM	Subscriber Identity Module
		SINR	Signal to Interference Noise Ratio
OS	Operating System	TBS	Transport Block Size
OSA	Optimized Service Aware	TDS	Time Domain Scheduler

TDMA	Time Division Multiple Access	VLR	Visitor Location Registry
TE	Terminal Equipment	VM	Virtual Machine
TTI	Transmission Time Interval	VMM	Virtual Machine Monitor
UE	User Equipment	VNet	Virtual Network
UL	Uplink		
UML	User Mode Linux	VNOs	Virtual Network Operators
UMTS	Universal Mobile Telecommunication System	VoIP	Voice over Internet Protocol
USIM	User Service Identity Module	WCDMA	Wideband Code Division Multiple Access
UTRAN	UMTS Terrestrial Radio Access Network	WLAN	Wireless Local Area Network

List of Symbols

Symbol	Meaning
α	smoothing factor
β	MCS scaling factor
$\overline{\gamma_k[t]}$	normalized average channel condition of bearer k
δ^2	variance
η	actual number of users served per TTI
θ_{max}	maximum achieved throughput if all PRBs are used under perfect channel conditions
$\theta_k[t]$	instantaneous achieved throughput for bearer k
$\overline{\theta_k[t]}$	normalized average throughout of bearer k
λ	arrival rate (file inter-arrival time)
$\mu(n)$	generic departure rate of state n
$\pi(n)$	state n steady state probability
$\boldsymbol{\pi}$	Markov chain steady state probability vector
τ	smoothing factor
ψ	maximum number of users served per TTI
$BLEP([\gamma_k])$	instantaneous Block Error Probability for channel state γ_k
$BLEP([\gamma_{eff}])$	instantaneous Block Error Probability for channel state γ_{eff}
$\overline{D}$	mean number of departures by unit time
E_{total}	total BE PRB estimate over all BE operators
$E(N)$	average required PRBs at the Nth TTI
F_i	operator i fairness factor
HOL_{delay_k}	head-of-line packet delay for bearer k
K	Number of MCSs
MCS_k	k^{th} modulation and coding scheme
n	Number of active users per TTI
n_k	number of users in MCS_k
N	Number of users in the system
N_0	thermal noise (dB)
NF	noise floor (dBm)

Symbol	Meaning
P_k	MCS_k static probability
P_L	path loss (dB)
P_{tx}	eNodeB transmission power per PRB (dBm)
$P_k^{BET}(t)$	BET scheduler time domain priority factor for bearer k
$P_k^{GBR}(t)$	time domain GBR priority metric of bearer k
$P_k^{MaxT}(t)$	MaxT scheduler time domain priority factor for user k
$P_k^{nonGBR}(t)$	time domain non-GBR priority metric of bearer k
$P_k^{w-BET}(t)$	weighted BET scheduler time domain priority factor for user k
$P_k^{w-MaxT}(t)$	weighted MaxT scheduler time domain priority factor for user k
$PRBsAlloc_i$	operator i allocated number of PRBs
$PRBsTTI(N)$	instantaneous PRB count at the Nth TTI
$\mathbf{Q}$	Markov chain infinitesimal generator matrix
$\overline{Q}$	mean number of users
R	distance between UE and eNodeB (km)
$S(n\delta)$	slow fading at point $n\delta$ (dB)
$SINR_{eff}$	effective SINR mapping
$SINR_k[t]$	instantaneous SINR value of bearer k
$SINR_{i,j}$	Signal to Interference Noise Ratio on PRB_i) for user j (dB)
$SINR_{max}$	scaling factor (maximum achieved SINR)
$t_{(\alpha/2,N-1)}$	upper critical value of the t-distribution with N-1 degrees of freedom
$\overline{t_{off}}$	traffic model average OFF duration
$\overline{t_{on}}$	average ON duration (file download time)
T_{avg}	average download time of all users
T_i	per-user average download time
$TBS_k(\eta)$	number of bits that can be transmitted by a served UE using MCS_k
$\overline{TBS}(n)$	state n average number of bits transmitted within a TTI
$\overline{TBS}(n_0,...,n_k)$	total bits sent by all served users under combination $(n_0,...,n_k)$
UF%	Unfairness factor (%)
V_i	i.i.d. normal random variable
W_{QoS_j}	QoS weight of the jth MAC QoS class
$\overline{x}$	sample mean
X_c	de-correlation distance (m)
$X_{k,i}$	scheduler decision whether a UE is served or not (1 or 0)
$\overline{X_{on}}$	traffic model average file size
$Z_{\alpha/2}$	upper $\alpha/2$ critical value of the standard normal distribution

1 Introduction

Long Term Evolution (LTE) is one of the latest releases of the Third Mobile Generation Partnership Project (3GPP). The idea behind standardizing LTE was to create a system that can surpass the older mobile standards (e.g., UMTS and HSPA), and stay competitive at least for the next 10 years. One of the main features of LTE is that it has a flat and IP packet based architecture. In addition, LTE standards define a new air interface that is based on the concept of Orthogonal Frequency Domain Multiple Access (OFDMA). Several QoS classes are supported in LTE, where services QoS requirements are guaranteed by defining the so called "bearer" concept. A bearer (EPS bearer) is an IP packet flow between the user side and the LTE core network with predefined QoS characteristics.

The LTE MAC scheduler is an important and crucial entity of the LTE system. It is responsible for efficiently allocating the radio resources among the different mobile users, who might have different QoS requirements. The scheduler design needs to take different considerations into account, for example, user throughput, QoS and fairness, in order to properly allocate the scarce radio resources. As mentioned earlier, LTE is a packet based system that adds several challenges in guaranteeing the QoS. In addition, LTE has a number of services each with their own QoS requirements. The scheduler has to be aware of the different service requirements and should try to satisfy all of them. Within this thesis a novel Optimized Service Aware scheduler (OSA) is proposed, implemented and investigated to address all of the aforementioned challenges. The OSA scheduler differentiates between the different QoS classes mainly by defining several MAC QoS bearer types, such as, Guaranteed (GBR) and non-Guaranteed (nonGBR) Bit Rate. At the same time, it gains from the multi-users-diversity by exploiting the different users' channel conditions in order to maximize the cell throughput. The OSA scheduler creates a balance between QoS guarantees and system performance maximization in a proportionally fair manner.

Another interesting research topic, which is discussed in this thesis, that is receiving immense attention in the research community is "Network Virtualization". Virtualization is a well known technique that has been used for years, especially in computing systems, e.g., use of virtual memory and virtual operating systems.

Nevertheless, the idea of using virtualization to create complete virtual networks is new. Looking at the Future Internet research one emerging trend is to have multiple coexisting architectures, in which each is designed and customized to fit one type of network with specific requirements. Network Virtualization will play a vital role in diversifying the Future Internet into, e.g., separate virtual networks that are isolated from each other, and can run different architectures within. In this thesis work a general framework for virtualizing the wireless medium is proposed and investigated. This framework focuses on virtualizing mobile communication systems so that multiple operators can share the same physical resources, while being able to stay isolated from each other. Although, the framework is applied to LTE, it can be generalized to fit other similar wireless system, e.g., WiMax. Several scenarios have been investigated to highlight the advantages that can be obtained from virtualizing the LTE system, more specifically virtualizing the air interface (i.e. spectrum sharing).

Simulations often take considerable time to run and produce results. In order to validate the simulation model, and to be able to produce results at a much faster pace, several analytical models have been proposed and developed by the author. The analytical models differentiate between three types of time domain schedulers: Maximum Throughput scheduler (MaxT), Blind Equal Throughput scheduler (BET), and Optimized Service Aware scheduler (OSA). The models are also split into two categories: One with no QoS differentiation, and another with QoS differentiation that can support two traffic classes.

The thesis work is organized as follows: Chapter 2 gives an introduction of the mobile communication history, with special focus on the 3rd Generation Partnership Project (3GPP) standards. It introduces first the second mobile generation, that is Global System for Mobile Communication (GSM), explaining the main features of GSM, as well as its network architecture and its main entities. Then, the third mobile generation, the Universal Mobile Telecommunication System (UMTS) is introduced, highlighting the main differences between UMTS and GSM. In addition, a short overview on UMTS extensions (i.e. High Speed Downlink Packet Access (HSDPA), and High Speed Uplink Packet Access (HSUPA)) is also given.

Chapter 3 introduces the Long Term Evolution (LTE), which is the main focus of this thesis. The main motivation and targets of LTE are explained, as well as the LTE radio related topics: e.g., the multiple access schemes used. Then, the LTE network architecture with each of the LTE entities and the protocols used in each are described in detail. In addition, the LTE quality of service bearer concepts are discussed. Finally, the chapter gives a short introduction on what is beyond LTE, i.e., LTE-advanced, explaining some of its main new features.

Chapter 4 describes the design and development of the detailed LTE network simulator developed in this thesis work. The LTE simulator is implemented using the OPNET simulation tool. This chapter describes the implemented nodes and their functionalities, as well as the developed channel model. Furthermore, this chapter explains the different traffic models used in this work with their corresponding parameters. Finally, the statistical evaluation methods used to perform the evaluations are explained.

Chapter 5 presents the network virtualization concept. The main focus of this chapter is the wireless virtualization of the LTE mobile system. A novel wireless virtualization framework, that is proposed by the author, is introduced and explained in detail. The work done in this chapter is part of the European project 4WARD [4WAf]. The objective of this chapter is to provide the concept of using wireless virtualization in LTE, and to highlight the potential gain in sharing the spectrum between several network operators, as well as the gain coming from the multi-user diversity exploitation. Several performance analyses are shown in this chapter highlighting the aforementioned gains.

Chapter 6 targets the design of an efficient and novel LTE radio scheduler. The proposed Optimized Service Aware scheduler (OSA) is explained in this chapter. The motivation of the OSA scheduler is to design a scheduler that can provide service differentiation, and guarantee the user Quality of Service (QoS), while at the same time provide good overall system performance. Several performance evaluations are discussed, comparing the OSA scheduler against other well known schedulers.

Chapter 7 presents the different novel LTE radio analytical models. Those models are based on the Continuous Time Markov Chain, and are extensions of the general analytical model presented in [DBMC10]. First, the general model of [DBMC10] is described, then the model adaptations and extensions to the LTE system are discussed. Two categories of analytical models are developed: one with no QoS differentiation, and the other with QoS differentiations. The results of these analytical models are compared against the simulation results.

Chapter 8 gives the overall conclusion of the thesis, highlighting all the main points and achievements. Finally, an outlook concerning future work is given.

2 Mobile Communication Systems

The first real wireless radio communication was used in the late of 1890s when Guglielmo Marconi demonstrated the first wireless telegraphy to the English telegraphy office. Then in the early 1900s he managed to successfully transmit radio signals across the Atlantic Ocean from Cornwall to Newfoundland [She00]. The first mobile communication systems started appearing later in the US during the 40s, and within Europe during the 60s.

In 1982 the Global System for Mobile Communication (GSM) specifications started with an objective of achieving a European mobile radio network that is digital and capable of handling roaming. This work on the specification continued until 1990, where the first phase of the GSM specification was frozen. The first official GSM network was deployed in Germany in 1992, and at the end of 1997 almost 98% of the population was reachable. GSM was a big success and spread very rapidly not only within Europe but all over the globe. GSM is also known as the 2nd generation cellular wireless system (2G).

In the 1980s the International Telecommunication Union (ITU) started specifying the next generation mobile communication system. The specifications were finalized by the end of the 1990s and this system was called International Mobile Telecommunication-2000 (IMT-2000). Then the 3GPP finalized the first version of their mobile communication system following GSM which was known as Universal Mobile Telecommunication System (UMTS).

In 2004 the 3GPP started working on the next mobile system which is called Long Term Evolution (LTE). The 3GPP releases overview with their release schedule can be seen in Figure 2.1. The 3GGP Specifications and their numbering schemes can be found in [3GP12].

Over the next subsections, a brief introduction of GSM and UMTS is given. As LTE is the main focus of this thesis, chapter 3 is reserved for the description of the LTE system.

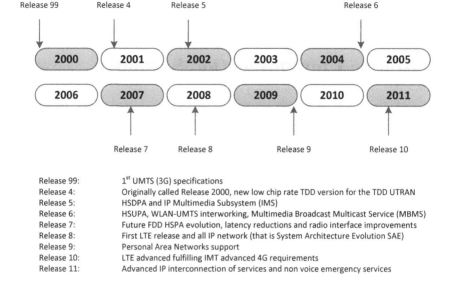

Figure 2.1: 3GPP releases overview [HT09] [Zah11]

2.1 Global System for Mobile Communication (GSM)

A mobile radio communication system by definition consists of telecommunication infrastructure serving users that are on the move (i.e., mobile). The communication between the users and the infrastructure is done over a wireless medium known as a radio channel. Telecommunication systems have several physical components such as: user terminal/equipment, transmission and switching/routing equipment, etc.

The GSM design has set the main basis and guidelines for all other mobile network generations to come. The GSM radio network consists of several radio cells each controlled by a Base Transceiver Station (BTS). A cell is a geographical representation of the coverage area within which a BTS can send and receive data. Cells are normally represented by hexagonal shapes for simplicity. Each base station serves a number of Mobile Stations (MS) representing the users, and a number of base stations are controlled by the Base Station Controller (BSC). The radio link from the BTS to the MS is known as Downlink (DL) and the other direction is known as Uplink (UL).

Figure 2.2 shows the general GSM network architecture. The GSM network architecture is divided into four main functional groups, these are:

- Mobile Station (MS): is also known as User Equipment (UE), this entity consists of the Subscriber Identity Module (SIM) and the terminal equipment.

- Base Station Subsystem (BSS): this entity handles the radio access functions, like radio resource management. It connects the UEs with the core network.

- Core Network (CN): includes the transport functions, mobility management, user/subscriber databases with their information, service controlling functions, billing, etc.

- External Network: these are the external networks that the UEs can communicate with and that the mobile network has to be connected to. It can be for example the public telephone network or any other GSM network.

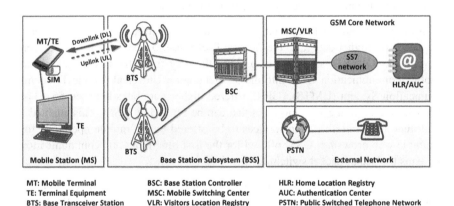

Figure 2.2: GSM network architecture [1]

---

[1]Picture is redrawn from http://en.wikipedia.org/wiki/GSM

One of the important features of a mobile communication system is the radio interface. A radio interface is the interface between the mobile stations and the base station. This interface enables the users of the mobile networks to be mobile with wireless access. The radio spectrum is the term used to describe the amount of resources (i.e., frequency bandwidth/spectrum) that the air interface uses. In mobile communication the radio spectrum is one of the most important parts due to its high incurring cost. In addition, the radio spectrum is often limited and is treated as a scarce resource that the users of the mobile communication system need to share. The sharing of the spectrum is done using the so-called *multiple access scheme*.

In GSM, a mixture of Time Division Multiple Access (TDMA) and Frequency Division Multiple Access (FDMA) is used as the multiple access scheme. FDMA is used to divide the GSM spectrum into several carrier frequencies. Each carrier frequency is then divided using TDMA into 8 time slots that are then used by the mobile stations for their transmissions. The maximum spectrum/frequency band of GSM is 25 MHz, that is 124 carrier frequencies that are separated from each other by 200 kHz. In GSM, Frequency Division Duplex (FDD) is also used to separate the downlink frequency range from the uplink.

GSM uses circuit switched techniques to support voice calls. Due to the emerging needs for higher data rates the General Packet Radio Service (GPRS) has been developed. GPRS is seen as a step along the way from the second generation mobile communication GSM into the 3rd generation Universal Mobile Telecommunication System (UMTS). GPRS offered higher data rates between 56 - 114 kbps compared to the very low rates that can be offered by GSM. This enabled a multitude of possibilities and services to be offered by the mobile operators, for example web browsing. GSM offered for the first time in mobile communication systems the use of packet switching.

After GPRS, the evolution of the GSM system kept going to support even higher data rates. This lead to the development of Enhanced Data for GSM Evolution (EDGE). The main feature of EDGE was that it enabled data rates up to 384 kbps, which is a significant improvement over GPRS. The increase in the data rate was achieved by changing the GSM modulation scheme from Gaussian Minimum Shift Keying (GMSK) to 8PSK[1]. Figure 2.3 shows the evolutions of the GSM system with their respective data rates.

---

[1] PSK stands for Phase Shift Keying.

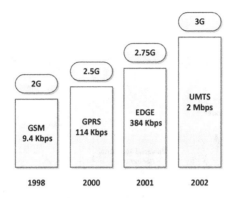

Figure 2.3: GSM system evolution

2.2 Universal Mobile Telecommunication System (UMTS)

The first version of the UMTS standards was finalized by the end of 1990, that is why UMTS is also sometimes referred to as release 99 or R99. The main motivation behind UMTS was to define a universal mobile communication standard that aims at higher peak rates, with the ability of dynamically adapting the user data rates. In addition, there were several other targets like the support of Quality of Service differentiation between the different new services offered by UMTS, as well as improving the overall spectral efficiency. UMTS uses Wideband Code Division Multiple Access (WCDMA) which is a completely new multiple access scheme compared to the one used in GSM. It also uses a larger bandwidth of 5 MHz for each of the downlink and uplink.

The UMTS architecture (Figure 2.4) is structured similarly to GSM with several modifications. The radio access network in UMTS is called UMTS Terrestrial Radio Access Network (UTRAN), and consists of Radio Network Controller (RNC) and several NodeBs (which represent the UMTS base stations). The UMTS network supports both circuit switched and packet switched connections. The circuit switched connections are used to carry voice services, whereas the packet switched connections are used for other data services, like web browsing through HTTP, and file downloads/uploads through FTP. More details related to UMTS can be found in [HT07].

Similar to GSM, two system enhancements have followed the UMTS system, to increase the data rates, increase the system capacity and reduce system latency.

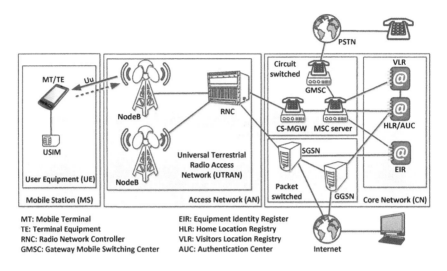

Figure 2.4: UMTS network architecture [1]

These two enhancements are represented by new 3GPP releases that is release 5 or High Speed Downlink Packet Access (HSDPA), and release 6 High Speed Uplink Packet Access (HSUPA).

HSDPA is already mentioned before the 5th release of the UMTS specification. The goal of this release was to enhance the downlink data rates of the UMTS standard up to 14 Mbps, increase the spectral efficiency, as well as reduce the system latency. This is achieved by the introduction of several new functions:

- Adaptive Modulation and Coding (AMC): in each user transmission the modulation and coding schemes is adaptively changed depending on the user channel conditions, for example, a user with very good channel conditions is assigned a higher modulation and coding scheme.

- Fast NodeB Scheduling: the scheduling function is moved from the RNC to the NodeB compared to GSM. Which means the NodeB can track the instantaneous channel changes of the users and schedule the resources in a more efficient way thus gaining from the multi-user diversity principle.

- Shorter Transmission Time Interval (TTI): the TTI length is reduced in HS-DPA to 2ms, instead of 10ms in UMTS R99. TTI is the duration of a trans-

---

[1]Picture is redrawn from http://en.wikipedia.org/wiki/UMTS

mission over the radio link, it is also the rate of the radio scheduler at which it takes decisions on which UEs transmit over the next TTI.

- Use of Hybrid Automatic Repeat Request (HARQ): performing retransmissions of the erroneous packets between the NodeB and the UE instead of waiting for higher layer retransmissions. This of course will result in latency reduction. In addition, chase combining and incremental redundancy are also used to combine the two unsuccessfully decoded packets with the new retransmission to improve the decoding probability.

Similar to HSDPA, HSUPA aims at enhancing the performance of the UMTS R99 uplink in terms of improving the user data rates up to 5.76 Mbps and reducing the latency. HSUPA also uses concepts similar to HSDPA: shorter 2ms TTI (optional), HARQ and fast scheduling. However, the AMC is not used in HSUPA since it does not support any high order modulation schemes and it only uses QPSK. This is because higher modulation schemes require more energy per bit resulting in faster battery discharge. In HSUPA, both soft and softer handover are allowed, unlike HSDPA, because the UE is the entity performing the transmission and the neighboring NodeBs can also listen to the UE transmission without any extra effort.

The use of both enhancements (i.e., HSDPA and HSUPA) is often referred to as HSPA. Network operators deploy HSPA in coexistence with R99 UMTS networks. The instantaneous radio performance may vary overtime, sometimes achieving very high cell throughputs. However, the network operators dimension their backhaul by considering the average performance so as to reduce cost [LZW+08], which will cause short term congestions in the network backhaul. In order to mitigate the influence of this, congestion control schemes as well as traffic separation techniques are used to overcome the aforementioned issues and provide QoS differentiation between HSPA and R99 traffic [WZTG+09] [LZW+10] [LWZ+11].

3 Long Term Evolution (LTE)

LTE is one of the newest releases of the 3rd Generation Partnership Project (3GPP) specifications. It is also referred to as 3.9G or Release 8. The 3GPP started working on LTE in November 2004 with the Radio Access Network (RAN) Evolution workshop in Toronto - Canada. The main task was to standardize a system with new design goals that can exceed older mobile standards (like UMTS and HSPA), as well as being able to stay competitive at least for the next 10 years.

3.1 Motivation and Targets

In March 2005, a feasibility study on LTE was launched. The main focus of this study was to decide what architecture the new system should have and what multiple access techniques were to be used. The LTE network architecture can be seen in Figure 3.1. The main conclusions drawn from the feasibility study [25.05] can be summarized in terms of requirements and targets as follows:

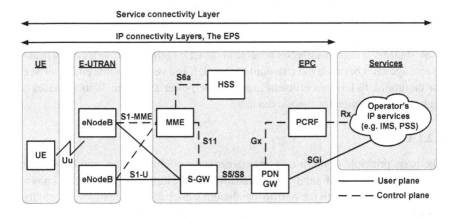

Figure 3.1: LTE EPS network architecture

- Simplified flat packet oriented network architecture

- High data rates up to 100 Mbps in the downlink and 50 Mbps in the uplink (even higher with Multi Input Multi Output (MIMO))

- Reduced latency

- Scalable usage of frequency spectrum from 1.25 MHz to 20 MHz

- OFDMA and SC-FDMA as the multiple access techniques for downlink and uplink respectively

3.2 LTE Multiple Access Schemes

In LTE the multiple access transmission scheme is based on the Frequency Domain Multiplexing (FDM). Two different versions are used: Orthogonal Frequency Domain Multiple Access (OFDMA) for the downlink, and Single Carrier Frequency Domain Multiple Access (SC-FDMA) for the uplink. OFDMA is a very efficient transmission scheme which is widely employed in many digital communication systems, e.g., Digital Video Broadcasting (DVB), WiMax, Wireless Local Area Network (WLAN). The reason behind the popularity of OFDMA comes from the fact that it has very robust characteristics against frequency selective channels. Frequency selectivity is one of the transmission problems that can be overcome through equalization, but the complexity of the equalization technique is very high. Another reason for choosing OFDMA as the downlink transmission scheme is the bandwidth flexibility it offers, since changing the number of sub-carriers used can increase or decrease the used frequency bandwidth.

SC-FDMA is the transmission scheme in the LTE uplink. It provides a low peak-to-average ratio between the transmitted signal; it is a very desirable characteristic for the uplink to have an efficient usage of the power amplifier. This provides a high battery life time for mobile devices.

3.2.1 OFDM

The basic principle of multi-carrier systems is the splitting of the total bandwidth into a large number of smaller and narrower bandwidth units, which are known as sub-channels. Due to the narrow bandwidth sub-channels frequency selectivity does not exist. As a result, only the gains of the sub-channels has to be compensated and no complex equalization techniques is required.

In OFDM the sub-channels are orthogonal to each other. This nice property does not require the addition of guard intervals between the sub-channels and hence it increases the system spectral efficiency. Figure 3.2 shows the orthogonality principle of OFDM; the frequency representation of one OFDM sub-channel is a Sinc[1] function, where if the sampling is done at the exact spacing the result will only be at the sub-carrier of that sub-channel and zeros at every other sub-carrier frequency. This means that the sub-channels are orthogonal to each other.

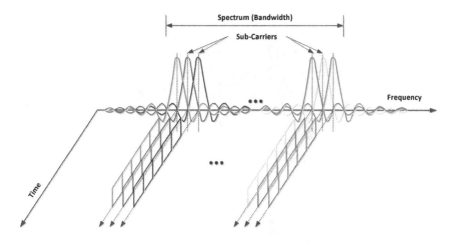

Figure 3.2: OFDM signal in frequency and time domain [Hoa05]

3.2.2 OFDMA

Orthogonal Frequency Division Multiple Access (OFDMA) is an access scheme that uses the OFDM principle to orchestrate the distribution of the scarce radio resources among several users enabling multi user communications. This is done by using the Time Domain Multiple Access (TDMA), where users dynamically get some resources at the different time instances of the scheduling.

The LTE MAC Scheduler (explained in chapter 6) makes use of the different user channel conditions to distribute the frequency resources (sub-carriers) to where it best fits. This can mean giving them to the users, for example with the best instantaneous channel conditions (Max-CI scheduling). This distribution process is determined by the used scheduler discipline.

---

[1]The sinc function, sometimes also known as the sampling function, is a function that is widely used in signal processing and Fourier transforms. It is commonly defined as $Sinc(x) = Sin(x)/x$.

Figure 3.3 shows an example of the channel dependent scheduling between two users, where the sub-carriers of the system are distributed between the two users based on who has the best channel. A system with such channel dependent scheduling is often very robust with a better system capacity and higher spectral efficiency than a single user OFDM system.

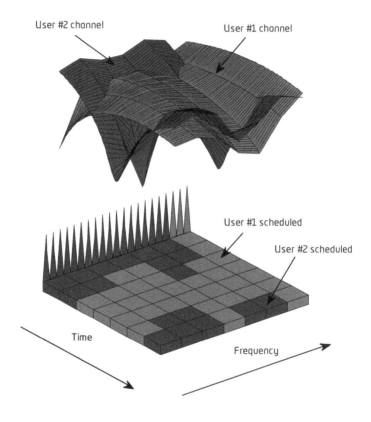

Figure 3.3: An example of channel dependent scheduling between two users [ADF⁺09]

3.2.3 SC-FDMA

As mentioned earlier, the Single Carrier Frequency Division Multiple Access is chosen as the transmission scheme for the LTE uplink. The motivation behind choosing SC-FDMA was the attractive characteristics it possesses, that is having a low peak to average ratio which is considered to be a very desired property for having efficient power amplifier that can save battery power of the mobile device for the uplink transmission.

SC-FDMA is a special type of OFDM that combines the low peak to average power ratio with multi path resistance and flexible and efficient frequency allocation. It still uses orthogonal sub-carriers similar to OFDMA, but with one difference, that is the sub-carriers used for transmission are chosen to be sequential and not in parallel. A small comparison between SC-FDMA and OFDMA can be seen in Figure 3.4.

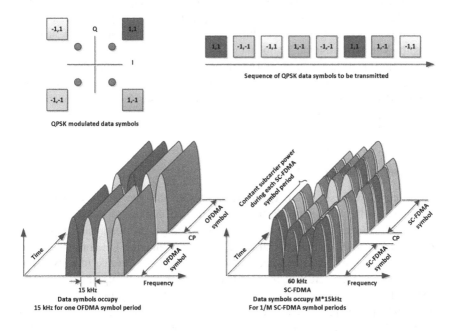

Figure 3.4: An example comparing SC-FDMA to OFDMA [Agi09]

3.3 LTE Network Architecture

The LTE system is designed for the packet switched services providing IP connectivity between the Packet Data Network (PDN) and the User Equipment (UE) without service interruption even during mobility. The LTE system can be divided into two main branches: Evolved Universal Terrestrial Radio Access Network (E-UTRAN) and System Architecture Evolution (SAE). The E-UTRAN evolved from the UMTS radio access network; it is sometimes also referred to as LTE. The SAE supports the evolution of the packet core network, also known as Evolved Packet Core (EPC). The combination of both the E-UTRAN and the SAE compose the Evolved Packet System (EPS). Figure 3.1 shows the general LTE network architecture.

According to [SBT09], an EPS bearer is defined to be an IP packet flow between the PDN-GW and the UE with predefined Quality of Service (QoS) characteristics. Both the EPC and the E-UTRAN are responsible for setting and releasing such a bearer depending on the application QoS requirements. In LTE multiple bearers can be established for users with multiple services, e.g., a user can have a voice call using the Voice over Internet Protocol (VoIP) and at the same time be downloading a file using File Transfer Protocol (FTP), or browse the web using the Hypertext Transfer Protocol (HTTP). Each of these services can be mapped to a different bearer. More detailed explanations on the quality of service and the bearers in LTE are given in section 3.5. In the next subsection a brief description of the important LTE nodes will be presented.

3.3.1 User Equipment (UE)

As the name suggests, a UE is the actual device that the LTE customers use to connect to the LTE network and establish their connectivity. The UE may take several forms; it can be a mobile phone, a tablet, or a data card used by a computer/notebook. Similar to all other 3GPP systems, the UE consists of two main entities: a SIM-card or what is also known as User Service Identity Module (USIM), and the actual equipment known as Terminal Equipment (TE). The SIM-card carries the necessary information provided by the operator for user identification and authentication procedures. The terminal equipment on the other hand provides the users with the necessary hardware (e.g., processing, storage, operating system) to run their applications and utilize the LTE system services.

3.3.2 Evolved UTRAN (E-UTRAN)

The E-UTRAN in LTE consists of directly interconnected eNodeBs which are connected to each other through the X2 interface and to the core network through the S1 interface. This eliminates one of the biggest drawbacks of the former 3GPP systems (UMTS/HSPA): the need to connect and control the NodeBs through the

Radio Network Controller (RNC), which make the system vulnerable to RNC failures. The LTE E-UTRAN architecture can be seen in Figure 3.5.

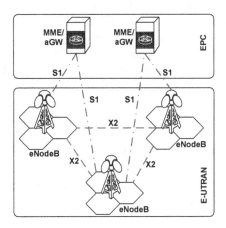

Figure 3.5: LTE E-UTRAN architecture

The enhanced NodeB (eNodeB) entity works as a bridge between the UE and the EPC. It provides the necessary radio protocols to the user equipment, so as to be able to send and receive data and it tunnels the users data securely over the LTE transport to the PDN-GW and vice versa. The GTP tunneling protocol is used, which works on top of the UDP/IP protocols. The eNodeB is also responsible for the scheduling which is one of the most important radio functions. The eNodeB schedules the frequency spectrum resources among the different users by exploiting both the time and frequency, while guaranteeing different quality of service for the end users. In addition, the eNodeB also has some mobility management functionalities, e.g., radio link measurements and handover signaling for other eNodeBs.

3.3.3 Evolved Packet Core (EPC)

As shown in Figure 3.1, the EPC (also known as the LTE core network) consists of three main entities: Mobility Management Entity (MME), Serving Gateway (S-GW) and the Packet Data Network Gateway (PDN-GW). In addition, there are some other logical entities like the Home Subscriber Server (HSS) and Policy and Charging Rules Function (PCRF). The main purpose of the EPC is to provide the necessary functionalities to support the users and establish their bearers [SBT09].

Each of the EPC main entities and their functionalities is described briefly in the next paragraphs. A more detailed description can be found in [36.11a]. The MME entity provides control functions as well as signaling for the EPC. The MME is only involved in the control plane. Some of the MME supported functions include: authentication, security, roaming, default/dedicated bearer establishment, tracking user mobility and handover. The S-GW is the main gateway for the user traffic, where all the users IP traffic goes through. It is the local mobility anchor point for inter-eNodeB handover, as well as the mobility anchoring for inter-3GPP mobility [36.11a]. In addition the S-GW provides several other functions like: routing, forwarding, charging/accounting information gathering. The packet data network gateway PDN-GW acts as the user connectivity point for the user traffic, it is responsible for assigning the users IP addresses as well as classifying the user traffic into different QoS classes. In addition, the PDN-GW acts as the mobility anchor point for inter-working with non 3GPP technologies, like Wireless LAN and WiMax.

3.4 E-UTRAN Protocol Architecture

The E-UTRAN protocols consist of both user plane and control plane. The user plane consists of a set of protocols used to transfer the actual user data through the LTE network, whereas the control plane consists of protocols which are used to control and establish the user connections and bearers within the E-UTRAN. Figure 3.6 shows the user plane protocol stack.

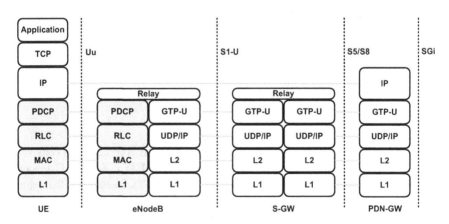

Figure 3.6: LTE E-UTRAN user plane protocol stack

The LTE radio access architecture is mainly the eNodeB which is an enhanced version of the original NodeB of the UMTS system. Since the RNC was removed from the LTE architecture some of its functions have been moved to the eNodeB. Figure 3.7 shows the detailed eNodeB and UE protocol architecture for the downlink [Dah07]. The main LTE radio interface protocols are [HT09]:

- Radio Resource Control (RRC): is responsible for the handover functions, like handover decisions, transfer of UE context from serving eNodeB to target eNodeB during handover. In addition, it controls the periodicity of the Channel Quality Indicator (CQI) and is also responsible for the setup and maintenance of the radio bearers [Mot].

- Packet Data Convergence Protocol (PDCP): is responsible for compressing the IP header, i.e., reduces the overall overhead which in turn improves the efficiency over the radio interface. This layer also performs additional functionalities, e.g., ciphering and integrity protection. A detailed description of the PDCP functionality can be found in [36.11c].

- Radio Link Control (RLC): is responsible for the segmentation and concatenation of the PDCP packets. It also performs retransmissions and guarantees in-sequence delivery of the packets to the higher layers. The RLC also performs error corrections using the well-known Automatic Repeat Request (ARQ) methods. A detailed description of the PDCP functionality can be found in [36.10b].

- Medium Access Channel (MAC): is responsible for scheduling air interface resources in both uplink and downlink. It is also responsible for satisfying the users' QoS over the air interface. In addition, the MAC layer also performs the Hybrid Automatic Repeat Request (HARQ).

- Physical Layer (PHY): is responsible for the radio related issues: e.g., modulation/demodulation, coding/decoding, Multi Input Multi Output (MIMO) techniques.

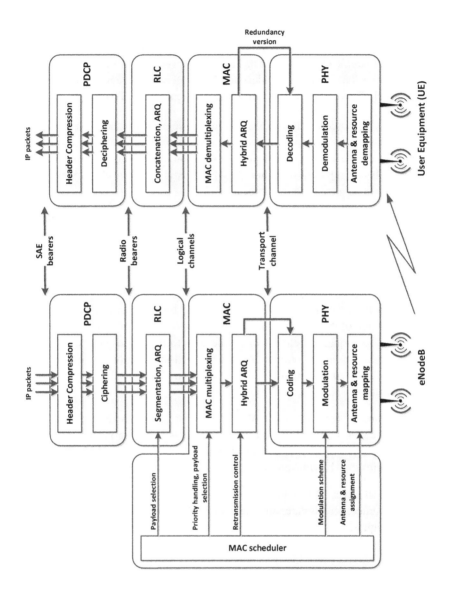

Figure 3.7: Detailed LTE downlink protocol architecture [Dah07]

3.4.1 Radio Link Control (RLC)

The radio link control protocol is responsible for the concatenation and segmentation process. It segments the packets that come from the PDCP layer (i.e., the IP packets after compressing the header) into smaller RLC packets, and concatenates the RLC packets on the receiver side into the PDCP packets. In addition to the above functionality, the RLC protocol provides reliable communication between the eNodeB and the UE by the aid of packet retransmissions. The RLC uses sequence numbers to detect lost packets at the receiver side and inform the sender which packets to retransmit by using some selective repeat retransmissions. This is also known as Automatic Repeat Request (ARQ). The RLC protocol can operate in three different operational modes, these are:

- Acknowledged Mode (AM): which is used to provide error-free transmission between sender and receiver. This mode is suitable for services that use the TCP transport protocol, like FTP and HTTP, where reliability and error free delivery is of the utmost importance.

- Unacknowledged Mode (UM): in this mode no retransmissions are performed and RLC only provides segmentation and concatenation functionalities. This mode is suitable for applications that does not require error-free transmission and can tolerate some losses, like VoIP and video conferencing.

- Transparent Mode (TM): this operation mode of RLC does not add any protocol overhead to the higher layer data. It can be used for example for random access.

The RLC segmentation and concatenation is done based on the MAC scheduler decision, where the scheduler informs the RLC layer on what Transport Block Size (TBS) to be used by a certain user/bearer. This tells the RLC the amount of bits to be sent down to the lower layer. In contrast to the RLC version used in UMTS/HSPA [ZWL$^+$08] [ZWL$^+$10], in LTE the RLC Packet Data Unit (PDU) size is not fixed and is dynamically changed based on the scheduler decision. In addition to the retransmission and segmentation/concatenation functionalities of RLC there are a number of other functionalities supported by RLC [HT07]:

- Padding

- In-Sequence delivery of higher layer PDUs

- Duplicate detection

- Flow control

- SN check (unacknowledged data transfer mode)

- Protocol error detection and recovery

- Ciphering

- Suspend/resume function for data transfer

3.4.2 Medium Access Control (MAC)

The MAC layer is responsible for one of the most important functionalities that is scheduling for both downlink and uplink. In addition, the MAC layer provides: Hybrid Automatic Repeat Request (HARQ), mapping between logical and transport channels, logical channel multiplexing/de-multiplexing, scheduling information reporting, priority handling between the UEs, priority handling between the logical channels on one UE, logical channel prioritization and transport format selection.

3.4.2.1 Logical and Transport Channels

As stated earlier, since the MAC layer is located below the RLC layer it provides services to the RLC by offering logical channels. Two different types of logical channels exist, these are traffic and control channels. This classification is done depending on the type of data the channel is transmitting. According to the 3GPP standards [36.11b], the logical channel types defined for the different kinds of services are listed in Table 3.1. The MAC layer uses the services offered by the physical layer in terms of using the Transport Channels. The LTE transport channels are listed in Table 3.2. A detailed description of the LTE logical and transport channels as well as how the mapping between them is done can be found in [Dah07].

Logical channel name	Acronym	Control channel	Traffic channel
Broadcast Control Channel	BCCH	X	
Paging Control Channel	PCCH	X	
Common Control Channel	CCCH	X	
Dedicated Control Channel	DCCH	X	
Multi-cast Control Channel	MCCH	X	
Dedicated Traffic Channel	DTCH		X
Multicast Traffic Channel	MTCH		X

Table 3.1: LTE MAC logical channels [36.11b]

Transport channel name	Acronym	Downlink	Uplink
Broadcast Channel	BCH	X	
Downlink Shared Channel	DL-SCH	X	
Paging Channel	PCH	X	
Multicast Channel	MCH	X	
Uplink Shared Channel	UL-SCH		X
Random Access Channel	RACH		X

Table 3.2: LTE MAC transport channels [36.11b]

3.4.2.2 HARQ

The hybrid ARQ is used by the MAC layer to provide reliable communication and to recover transmission errors. The HARQ mechanisms used in LTE are similar to the ones used before in HSPA. A multiple stop-and-wait process protocol is used for the HARQ (shown in Figure 3.8), where the sender sends the packets and the receiver gets those packets and tries to decode them and check if they are corrupted or not. Then the receiver can report back to the sender; if the decoding was successful or not by sending either an Acknowledgment (ACK) or a negative Acknowledgment (NAK).

In LTE, two different protocols are used for the HARQ [Dah07] depending whether it's an uplink or downlink transmission. For the downlink transmission an asynchronous protocol is used, where the retransmissions can happen at any time and that is why the process number has to be used so as to explicitly identify which process is being handled. As for the uplink transmission, a synchronous protocol is used to handle the retransmissions without the need to have the explicit process number. The retransmission is done based on a fixed time interval that both the sender and the receiver know.

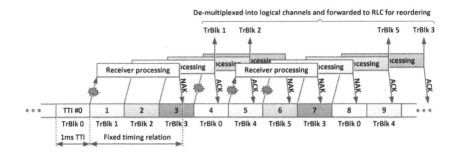

Figure 3.8: Multiple parallel HARQ processes example [Dah07]

Looking back at the RLC functionalities described earlier, it can be noticed that a retransmission scheme similar to the MAC HARQ one is also used. Although this might look like using redundant mechanisms, nevertheless, it is important to have both operating on top of each other. The reason is that although the MAC HARQ handles the errors due to the erroneous channel it still fails in some cases, for example, when a NAK is mistakenly assumed to be a positive acknowledgment due to some channel errors. This would lead to the RLC layer receiving packets with gaps between the in-sequence packets and if there is no ARQ functionality within the RLC layer to recover these missing packets then TCP will have to handle the missing packets. TCP treats all missing packets as an indication of congestion, which will lead to the activation of the TCP congestion avoidance functionality, and thus causes an unnecessary reduction of the overall throughput.

3.4.2.3 Scheduling

Scheduling in LTE is one of the integral functionalities of the MAC layer. The main purpose of the scheduling is how to orchestrate the user access to the shared transport data channels, that is the DL-SCH and UL-SCH.

LTE uses OFDMA as the basic access transmission scheme over the air interface. This means that there are two dimensions to the resources that are to be scheduled: time and frequency dimension. The task of the scheduler is to distribute these resources dynamically between the different users and their services depending on a number of criteria: e.g., Channel conditions, Quality of Service (QoS) and fairness.

The scheduler dynamically decides which users are to be scheduled within each Transmission Time Interval (TTI). Where multiple users can share the transport channel and transmit data within each TTI. The scheduler distributes the Physical Resource Blocks (PRBs) between the different users. A PRB is the smallest resource the scheduler can allocate (described in 3.4.3). In LTE, the MAC scheduling is divided into two independent scheduling algorithms, one for the downlink and one of the uplink. These two algorithms share some similar features but some structural differences still exist between the two regarding functionality, and that is because both schedulers are actually located at the MAC layer of the eNodeB.

The LTE MAC scheduler is one of the basic topics within this thesis. A detailed explanation of the different mechanisms and functionalities of the scheduler will be presented in chapter 6.

3.4.3 LTE Frame and Physical Resource Structure

As explained earlier, the resources in LTE consist of both time and frequency dimension. These resources as shown in Figure 3.9 are structured in the following manner [SBT09]:

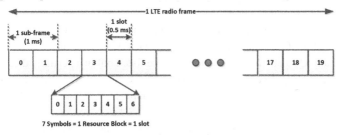

Figure 3.9: LTE FDD frame structure [Anr09]

First of all, the largest unit within the LTE hierarchical resources structure is the LTE radio frame. It is a 10ms radio frame that is divided into ten smaller 1ms sub-frames. Now, each sub-frame is further divided into two time slots with 0.5ms duration. These 0.5 ms time slots consist of 7 OFDM symbols in the time domain and groups of 12 sub-carriers in the frequency domain. The smallest modulation structure in LTE is the Resource Element. A Resource Element has one sub-carrier in the frequency domain and one symbol in the time domain. A slot of 7 OFDM symbols and 12 sub-carriers is normally known as a Physical Resource Block (PRB). A PRB is the smallest unit that the MAC scheduler can allocate to a user. Figure 3.10 shows the relationship between several frame elements.

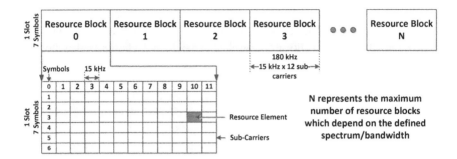

Figure 3.10: Relationship between slot, symbol and resource blocks [Anr09]

3.5 LTE Quality of Service Bearers

Quality of service is a well-known concept within the 3GPP systems, it can be found in legacy 3GPP standards like UMTS/HSPA. Within these previous 3GPP releases many QoS attributes and parameters existed but in a partially disconnected manner from the application layer. This had led to some difficulties in setting and configuring these parameters in the correct manner to achieve the desired QoS targets.

In SAE, and to avoid all of the previously mentioned issues it was agreed to reduce the number of the QoS parameters and define them with very clearly defined characteristics. Thus, an EPS bearer was defined to enable the EPS to guarantee the QoS of a certain traffic flow between the PDN gateway and the UE. A bearer is defined to be the basic element with the LTE QoS support concept. The basic SAE bearer model is shown in Figure 3.11. It can be seen that different bearers types have been defined between the different elements of the LTE network. The end-to-end service, which is normally between the two communicating end nodes, is divided into external bearer and an EPS bearer which is further divided into S5/S8 bearer, S1 bearer and radio bearer.

Within today's mobile communication usage, people use multiple services at the same time each of which has different QoS requirements. Users can make a phone call using a VoIP service, and browse the Internet or download/upload a file at the same time. Looking at these services some have much higher strict requirements than others, VoIP for example needs a very low delay and jitter, whereas web browsing and FTP downloads/uploads can tolerate much higher delays than

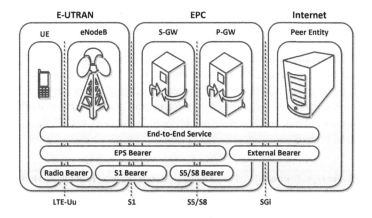

Figure 3.11: SAE bearer model [HT09]

VoIP. In order to distinguish between these services and guarantee their QoS requirements different bearers are set up by the EPS each with a different QoS association.

From the literature, two main general categories are defined in classifying the bearers, depending on the type of QoS they need to satisfy and these are:

- Guaranteed Bit Rate bearers (GBR): these bearers, as the name suggests, guarantee a minimum bit rate for their services. These bearers carry an associated value that allow other units to reserve/allocate resources for them. Such bearers can be used for applications, like VoIP or video conferencing.

- Non-Guaranteed Bit Rate bearers (non-GBR): these bearers do not guarantee any bit rate and are a kind of best effort service. No resources are pre-allocated or reserved for these bearers and they are served only if there are resources/bandwidth left for them. Such bearers can be used for applications like HTTP (web browsing) or file transfers like FTP downloads/uploads.

The eNodeB is the entity responsible for guaranteeing the QoS requirements of the bearers over the radio part. Each bearer is associated with two QoS parameters [SBT09], and these are:

- QoS Class Identifier (QCI): this is an index that identifies predefined values for priority, delay budget and packet loss rate. Each bearer carries this value

and the eNodeB reads this value and determines how to handle this bearer.
A number of QCIs are standardized and are listed in Table 3.3.

• Allocation and Retention Priority (ARP): this parameter defines the importance of bearer request establishment. It is used to determine whether to
  accept or reject a bearer establishment in case of radio congestion. This
  parameter is only used during bearer setup and doesn't influence other decisions once the bearer has been established, i.e., it does not affect scheduling
  or rate control.

QCI	Bearer type	Priority	Packet delay budget (ms)	Packet error loss rate	Example services
1	GBR	2	100	10^{-2}	Conversational voice
2	GBR	4	150	10^{-3}	Conversational video (live streaming)
3	GBR	5	300	10^{-6}	Non-conversational video (buffered streaming)
4	GBR	3	50	10^{-3}	Real time gaming
5	non-GBR	1	100	10^{-6}	IMS signaling
6	non-GBR	7	100	10^{-3}	Voice, video (live streaming), interactive gaming
7	non-GBR	6	300	10^{-6}	Video (buffered streaming)
8	non-GBR	8	300	10^{-6}	TCP based (e.g., www, e-mail, chat, FTP, p2p)
9	non-GBR	9	300	10^{-6}	

Table 3.3: LTE standardized QCIs and their parameters [SBT09]

3.6 Beyond LTE

Up to now, this chapter has presented and discussed the 3GPP Long Term Evolution (LTE). However, according to [PDF+08] the focus now is gradually shifting
from LTE (as the work on the first release of the LTE standard is coming to an
end) towards the LTE-advanced. LTE-advanced is the evolution of the LTE system that targets the enhancements of the LTE system so as to meet and exceed the
IMT-Advanced requirements within the ITU-R time plan [Nak09]. LTE-advanced
targets much higher data rates compared to LTE, as well as enhancing the spectrum efficiency. Table 3.4 shows a comparison between LTE, LTE-advanced and

the IMT-advanced systems. For the IMT-advanced system the 1 Gbps peak data rate shown in the table is only for low mobility cases, whereas it will support 100 Mbps for the high mobility cases.

		LTE	LTE-advanced	IMT-advanced
Peak data rate	DL	300 Mbps	1 Gbps	1 Gbps
	UL	75 Mbps	500 Mbps	
Peak spectrum	DL	15	30	15
efficiency (bps/Hz)	UL	3.75	15	6.75

Table 3.4: System performance comparison [Nak09]

Some of the main requirements considered in LTE-advanced include [Nak09]: wider bandwidth for transmission and spectrum sharing, advanced multi-antenna (MIMO) solutions, coordinated multi-point transmission and reception (CoMP) and the use of Relays and Repeaters. Over the next subsections each of these requirements is explained briefly.

3.6.1 Wider Bandwidth for Transmission

LTE-advanced is designed to operate in different spectrum allocations, that can be wider than the 20 MHz spectrum in which LTE operates. Although it is very favorable to have the wider spectrum, it is very difficult within today's free spectrum to find this. That is why, the IMT-advanced specifications have enabled the use of bandwidth aggregation to meet the current demands of higher spectrum.

In LTE-advanced, a technique called *Carrier Aggregation* (CA) is used to provide the necessary means to combine bandwidths to provide the wider operating spectrum. According to [Agi11], three main carrier aggregation scenarios are supported: intra-band contiguous, intra-band non-contiguous, and inter-band non-contiguous aggregation.

3.6.2 Advanced MIMO Solutions

In LTE, the use of multiple antennas has been defined and used for both downlink and uplink transmissions. In the downlink transmission it is allowed to use a maximum of 4 spatial layers of transmission, whereas, in the uplink only one layer of transmission is allowed.

In LTE-advanced, the number of spatial layers has been increased in comparison to LTE. It is permitted to use up to eight layers in the downlink and four layers in the uplink [Agi11]. Increasing the number of transmission layers improves the user peak data rates because of the enhanced spatial multiplexing.

3.6.3 CoMP

Coordinated multi-point is an advanced MIMO technique used to improve the system coverage, cell-edge throughput and system efficiency. The concept behind CoMP is simple, when the user is in the cell edge, in the downlink, the user can receive the signals coming from multiple eNodeBs, whereas in the uplink the multiple eNodeBs can receive the user's transmission. Now, if the downlink transmission of the multiple eNodeBs are coordinated, a significant improvement in the overall performance can be achieved. In LTE-advanced, the CoMP transmission is used in the downlink, whereas, the CoMP reception is used in the uplink. Figure 3.12, shows the LTE-advanced CoMP concept.

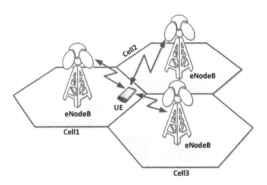

Figure 3.12: LTE-advanced CoMP

3.6.4 Relays and Repeaters

Relaying is used in order to deploy cells in areas where no (or very expensive) wired backhaul exists. It is often used to improve the coverage and throughput, for example, in urban, and rural scenarios. Figure 3.13 shows a typical scenario where a Relay Node (RN) is connected to an eNodeB wirelessly. The eNodeB that the RN is connected to is called in that case, a Donor eNodeB (DeNB). According to [Agi11], there are two main proposals for 3GPP release 10 (LTE-advanced) on how the RN connects to the DeNB, and these are:

- In-band: where the link between the RN and the UE uses the same carrier frequency of the link between the RN and the DeNB.

- Out-band: where the two links (RN<->UE and RN<->DeNB) do not use the same carrier frequency.

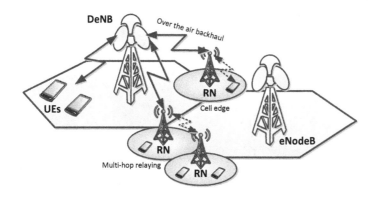

Figure 3.13: LTE-advanced in-band relay and backhaul [Agi11]

4 LTE Network Simulator

4.1 Simulation Environment

The LTE simulation model developed in this work is implemented using the OP-NET software environment [mod11]. OPNET is a commercial simulation tool that provides several network and application performance management solutions. The simulation modeling tool of OPNET Modeler© is used to design and implement the LTE simulation model. It is a hierarchical modeling environment that is based on a C/C++ programming tool, and has an advanced Graphical User Interface used for analysis and debugging. Some of its key features include [mod11]: a model library involving many protocols and vendor nodes implementations, object oriented programming, a 32-bit and 64-bit fully parallel simulation kernel. As stated earlier, it consists of several hierarchical editors as shown in Figure 4.1 mainly: project editor, node editor, process editor and open model source code.

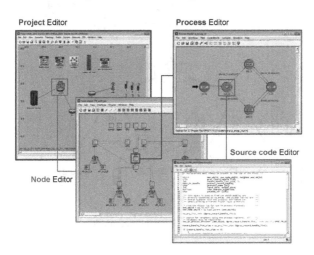

Figure 4.1: OPNET modeler© hierarchical editors

4.2 Simulation Framework

The main objective behind the development of the LTE simulation model is to analyze, evaluate and study several aspects of the LTE network such as: end user performance, LTE radio performance (Uu interface) and the LTE transport performance (S1/X2 interface). To be able to achieve the above targets the simulation model is designed to model both the E-UTRAN and EPC. The modeling is done with particular focus on the important features and functionalities of the nodes and protocols. These are modeled with great depth in order to be able to conduct the intended study. Mobile communication systems are very complex and include a huge amount of functionalities; this is also the case with LTE. To simplify the modeling of such a system, a reference architecture is required that represents the desired compromise between the complexity and the intended simulation performance targets. The reference LTE network architecture used for this thesis is shown in Figure 4.2 [Wee11]. It consists of a number of eNodeBs each controlling three cells. The number of eNodeBs, intermediate routers and users shown in the figure are merely an example and can be changed depending on the required scenario.

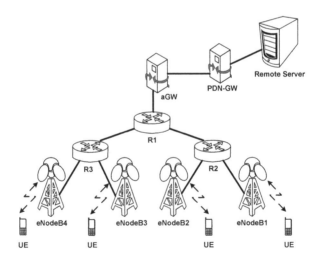

Figure 4.2: LTE reference model

By comparing the reference architecture to the general LTE network architecture shown on Figure 3.1, it can be seen that most of the entities have been modeled and implemented with special focus on the data plane. The reference architecture consists of a remote server representing an end communicating node somewhere in the Internet, the PDN-GW and the aGW representing the EPC part, and finally the eNodeBs and the UEs representing both the E-UTRAN and the UE part.

4.3 Simulation Model

By considering the LTE reference network architecture, the LTE OPNET node model can be seen in Figure 4.3. A simulation model is implemented in the thesis in accordance with the LTE 3GPP specifications [ZWGTG11a]. This simulation model is a completely new implementation and is not the same LTE model that comes with the OPNET installation. The implemented model holds more detailed modeling of specific functionalities that the default OPNET model does not model, e.g., a full MAC scheduler implementation.

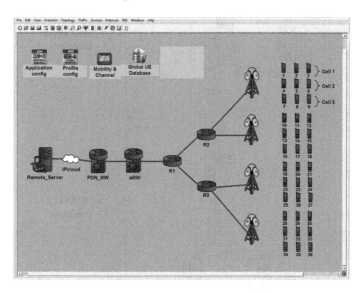

Figure 4.3: LTE OPNET simulation model

The numbers of eNodeBs, UEs, transport routers shown in the figure are merely examples, and the model is generic enough to configure any number of nodes and constellations, which is only limited by the system memory. Over the next subsections, each one of these nodes will be explained in detail. First, the main implemented LTE nodes, that is the UE, eNodeB, aGW, and PDN gateway are explained in sections 4.3.1 to 4.3.4. Then, the supporting nodes represented by the mobility and channel model node, and the global user database are explained in sections 4.3.5 and 4.3.6. Finally, in sections 4.3.7 and 4.3.8 the standard OPNET configurations nodes are explained.

4.3.1 UE Node Model

The UE node model can be seen in Figure 4.4. This node represents the user equipment with its predefined protocols, according to the 3GPP standard. These protocols include: application layer, (TCP, UDP)/IP, PDCP, RLC, MAC, and PHY.

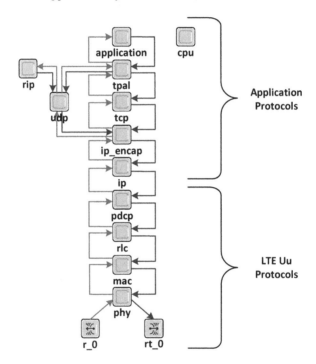

Figure 4.4: UE node model

This UE node also holds the individual user attributes, for example, the user speed, the serving eNodeB, the serving cell and the user applications. The emulation of the physical layer and the wireless medium is handled by the MAC layer with the physical layer using the well known Link-to-System level interface (L2S) and the Additive White Gaussian Noise (AWGN). The detailed explanation of this process is given later in chapter 6 within the MAC scheduler description.

4.3.2 eNodeB Node Model

The eNodeB is the node connecting the UEs to the transport network, and thus includes all the required protocols from both sides. This means the eNodeB includes the radio interface protocol, so as to be able to communicate with the UEs, and it includes the transport protocols, in order to tunnel the user data to the LTE core network. Figure 4.5 shows the eNodeB node model with all the aforementioned protocols.

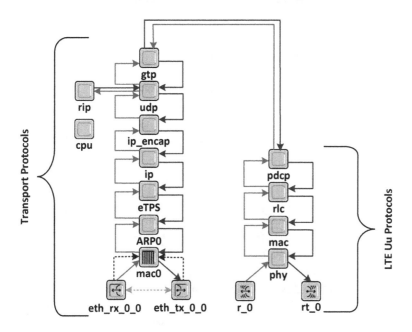

Figure 4.5: eNodeB node model

As shown in Figure 4.5, the radio interface protocols, which are the counter part of the UE radio protocols include: PHY, MAC, RLC and PDCP. The transport protocols include: GTP, UDP/IP and Ethernet. The service differentiation is done at the eNodeB. The eNodeB acts as the tunneling end point for the downlink traffic coming from the aGW. As for the uplink, the eNodeB tunnels the users' uplink traffic to the aGW. The MAC schedulers, both the downlink and the uplink, are implemented at the eNodeB MAC layer. Since the MAC scheduler is an integral part of this work, chapter 6 is dedicated for its detailed explanation.

4.3.3 Access Gateway Node Model

The aGW node model is shown in Figure 4.6. This node acts as the tunneling end point for both the downlink traffic coming from the PDN-GW and for the uplink traffic coming from the eNodeB. This means that the aGW node connects the transport from one side and the core network from the other side. The protocols implemented in the aGW include: GTP, UDP/IP and Ethernet.

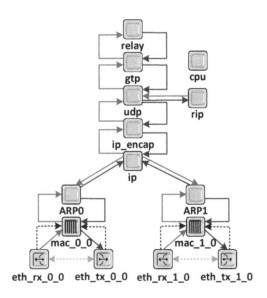

Figure 4.6: aGW node model

4.3.4 Packet Data Network Gateway Node Model

The PDN-GW, as the name suggests, is the gateway of the LTE system to the outside world. It connects the E-UTRAN to the external remote server. The PDN-

GW node model is shown in Figure 4.7. As seen in the figure, the node tunnels the original downlink IP packets coming from the server to the aGW. This is done by having the IP address of the PDN-GW as the destination address of the downlink traffic coming from the server, and then the packets are forwarded to the relay node (acting as the upper layer above IP) which starts the tunneling of the data by addressing it to the aGW. As for the uplink traffic, the tunneled data coming from the aGW is de-tunneled at the relay node to the original IP packets of the users, which are forwarded immediately to the ARP layer and then to the remote server (simplified modeling). The PDN-GW has several Ethernet interfaces that connect the LTE core network with other 3GPP and non-3GPP networks.

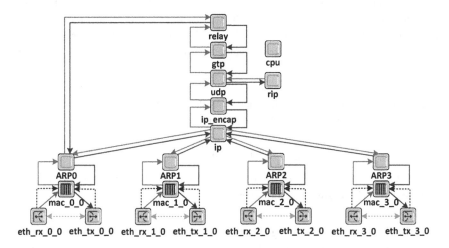

Figure 4.7: PDN-GW node model

4.3.5 Mobility and Channel Node

This node includes the implementation of both the mobility models as well as the channel models. The mobility and channel model are implemented together in one node because the channel model depends on the user position and thus its mobility. The mobility model emulates the user movement within the cell by updating the user's location at every sampling interval, which has been adaptively configured according to the UE speed. Two different mobility models have been implemented with the LTE simulation model, these are: Random Way Point (RWP) [CBD02] and Random Direction (RD) [CBD02]. All UE mobility information are stored and updated regularly in the global user database, where it can be accessed at any time by any node in the system. Details of these mobility models can be found in Appendix A.1.

The users channel conditions are updated in regular time intervals. The channel conditions consist of the three well known effects, these are: path loss, slow fading and fast fading. The sum of all the three factors results in the overall losses (in dB) between the user and the eNodeB. LTE operates in a scalable range of spectrum starting from 1.4 MHz all the way up to 20 MHz, and the spectrum itself is divided into Physical Resource Blocks (PRB). A PRB is the smallest unit the MAC scheduler can allocate to a specific user. The path loss, slow fading and fast fading are calculated for each user over each PRB. By using the link budget the Signal to Interference plus Noise Ratio (SINR) of each PRB maybe calculated for each user. The PRBs of each user have different values mainly due to the frequency and time selectivity.

Path Loss: The path loss is modeled by following the distance dependent path loss model given by the 3GPP [25.06] as follows:

$$P_L = 128.1 + 37.6 \times log_{10}(R) \tag{4.1}$$

where P_L is the path loss factor in dB. R represents the distance between the user and the eNodeB measured in kilometers.

Slow Fading: The slow fading is typically modeled using a log normal distribution with zero mean and a constant variance, but the time correlation between the slow fading values needs to be considered. For such a model, a moving mobile user starting at an initial point P, where the slow fading value is to be randomly generated using the log-normal distribution equal to $S(0)$. The shadowing at points which are at distance δ, 2δ, 3δ away from P can be determined according to [CYG95] as follows:

$$S(n\delta) = S((n-1)\delta) \times e^{-\delta/X_c} + V_i \tag{4.2}$$

where $S(n\delta)$ represents the slow fading value at a distance $n\delta$ away from point P, X_c is the de-correlation distance, and V_i are independent and identically distributed normal random variables with zero mean, and a variance equal to:

$$\delta_2^2 = \delta^2 \left[1 - e^{-2\delta/X_c} \right] \tag{4.3}$$

Fast Fading: The fast fading is implemented using a Jakes-like method, which can be found in [Val06] [LV08b] [KSK$^+$08]. It models Doppler spread for the time selectivity and the delay spread for frequency selectivity. As a result, a correlated time and frequency domain fast fading model is created. In contrast to the path loss and slow fading, the fast fading is different for each PRB of each user since the channel is frequency selective. Figure 4.8 shows the channel gain in dB using the Jakes-like method.

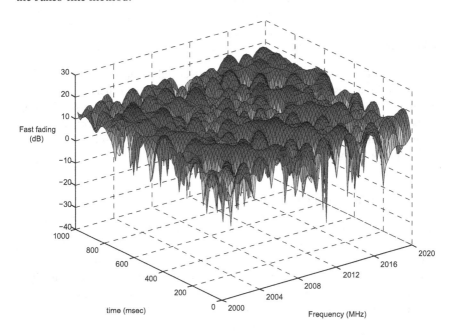

Figure 4.8: An example result of the fast fading model

Once the total losses are calculated, the SINR per PRB for each user is calculated using the link budget formula as follows:

$$SINR_{i,j} = P_{tx} - TotalLosses_{i,j} - NF - N_0 \qquad (4.4)$$

where $SINR_{i,j}$ is the SINR value on PRB_i for user j, P_{tx} is the eNodeB transmission power per PRB (here the total power is assumed to be equally distributed between the PRBs), TotalLosses are the summation of the three individual loss components (path loss, slow fading and fast fading), NF is the noise floor and N_0 is the thermal noise. The eNodeB transmit power is chosen in such a way that even the cell-edge users (with the lowest Modulation and Coding Scheme (MCS)) are able to transmit. For example, if we assume a transmit power of 20dBm for a system with 20MHz bandwidth and 100 PRBs then the transmit power per PRB under the equal power distribution assumption is:

$$20dBm - 10log_{10}\left(100PRBs\right)dBm = 0dBm \equiv 1mW \qquad (4.5)$$

4.3.6 Global User Database

The global user database is implemented to collect and update the global information of all the nodes of the system (including the UEs) upon their changes. For example, if users change their position during the mobility then this information is updated in the global database. In addition, all other related information e.g., channel conditions are updated accordingly. This information within this node is accessible for all the other nodes in the system.

4.3.7 Application Configuration

This is a standard OPNET node that is used to configure the different application parameters. It includes several supported applications, e.g., Email, FTP, HTTP, Video Conferencing, Voice, as well as other custom applications. Each one of these supported applications contains several parameters that can be configured with different supported distributions, e.g., exponential, Pareto, constant, normal etc. This application configuration is used later by the profile configuration to configure a certain user application profile.

Figure 4.9: Sample OPNET application configuration

Figure 4.9 shows a sample OPNET configuration window for an FTP application, it can be seen that the file size is constant (15Mbyte), and the inter-arrival time between the files is also constant (1 sec).

4.3.8 Profile Configuration

The OPNET profile configuration, is used to define a certain user application profile. It is always used in combination with the application configuration. A profile is a collection of one or several applications that a certain user can be configured to run. Within the profile configuration each application start and finish time can be set, as well as its repeatability. A profile configuration example can be seen in Figure 4.10.

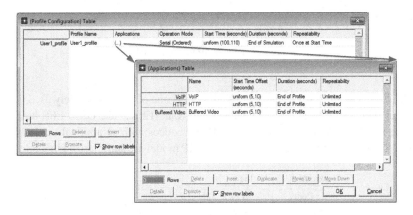

Figure 4.10: Sample OPNET profile configuration

4.4 Traffic Models

One of the key issues in simulating a communication network is knowing the traffic types and services that the network is carrying. Therefore, finding the correct traffic models to implement in the network simulator is a crucial part in the modeling, so as to have a meaningful evaluation. In this section, several traffic models including Voice over Internet Protocol (VoIP), Web traffic, Video traffic and File Transfer Protocol (FTP) are discussed.

4.4.1 Voice over IP Model (VoIP)

As discussed earlier, LTE is a packet based network. This means circuit switched voice traffic is not used anymore, and all voice data has to be sent over a packet network. Thus, the QoS should be guaranteed. The VoIP traffic is modeled using an ON/OFF model [Li10] that models the active and silent periods as seen in Figure 4.11.

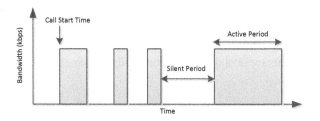

Figure 4.11: VoIP traffic model

The encoder used for the VoIP traffic model is one of the most widely used voice codecs that deploys the GSM Enhanced Full Rate (EFR). The GSM EFR belongs to the family of Adaptive Multi-Rate (AMR) codecs with an application data rate of 12.2 kbps. The main parameters of the VoIP model are summarized in Table 4.1.

Parameter	Value
Voice Codec	GSM EFR with 12.2 kbps data rate
Silence period	Exponential distribution with mean 3 seconds
Talk period	Exponential distribution with mean 3 seconds

Table 4.1: VoIP traffic model parameters [Li10]

In order to properly evaluate the performance of the VoIP traffic, the Mean Opinion Score (MOS) is used [IT09]. MOS measures the subjective quality of a voice call and returns a scalar one digit score to express the status of the call quality. The MOS score ranges from 1 (unacceptable call quality) up to 5 (excellent call quality) as shown in Figure 4.12. MOS values that are larger than 4 correspond to users being satisfied with their VoIP quality [Vi10].

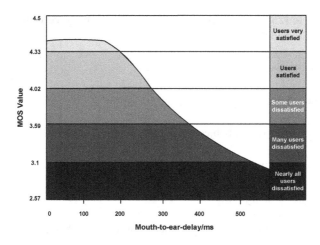

Figure 4.12: VoIP MOS values [IT09]

4.4.2 Web Browsing Model

A typical web browsing session consists of ON/OFF traffic periods that are separated by reading times as seen in Figure 4.13 [25.04]. The model represents the human behavior, where at first the web request is made by the user and then the requested web page along with all embedded objects are transferred to the terminal. Once the whole page is received the user will need time to read the page before the next request is made. This time is the so-called user reading time which needs to be considered in the traffic modeling.

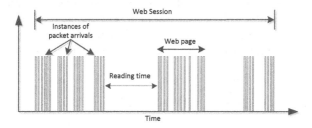

Figure 4.13: Web traffic model

According to [25.04], several random variables are required to model the web browsing traffic and these are:

- Main object size

- Embedded object size

- Number of embedded objects in a page

- Page reading time

- Main page parsing time

The basic web browsing model parameters used in this thesis are:

Parameter	Value
Number of pages per session	constant 5 pages
Average page size	constant 100 kbyte
Number of objects in a page	2 objects: 1 kbyte and 100 kbyte
Reading time	constant 12 seconds
Protocol	HTTP with each page using a separate TCP connection

Table 4.2: Web browsing traffic model parameters [Wee11]

4.4.3 Video Streaming Model

The video traffic model used in this thesis represents a buffered video streaming service. The basic model is simplified in such a way that the application layer generates video frames with inter-arrival time between the frames and then these frames are carried over the LTE transport network using the UDP transport protocol. The two main random variables that can be configured for the video source are:

- **Frame size**: this is the actual frame size in bytes

- **Frame inter arrival time**: the time between two consecutive video frames. This time is between the start of the last video frame and the start of the next one

4.4.4 File Transfer Model

The File Transfer Protocol application consists of a sequence of file transfers. It is similar to the web browsing application with the difference that it only transfers one large file compared to several smaller objects (in case of HTTP). FTP, like the HTTP web browsing, relies on TCP as the underlying protocol for the data transmission. An FTP session can be configured using only two random variables [25.04]:

- **FTP File Size**: that is the actual application file size that needs to be transmitted

- **Reading time**: the time between two consecutive FTP file transfers. This time starts after the finish of the previous FTP file

4.5 Statistical Evaluation

So far, this chapter has discussed the methodology and implementation assumptions used for building the LTE simulation model. However, the main reason why a simulation model is developed in the first place is to study and analyze the end-to-end system performance. This is done by collecting several statistical data and analyzing them. The results mainly focus on the steady state analysis, in which the average value is presented along with the "Confidence Interval", which is the widely used statistical method to indicate the sample mean error.

4.5.1 Confidence Interval Estimation

According to [Per09], having N consecutive endogenously obtained observations of a random variable, i.e. $x_1, x_2, x_3, x_4, ...x_N$, the sample mean of that random variable $\bar{x}$ can be calculated as:

$$\bar{x} = \frac{1}{N} \sum_{i=1}^{n} x_i \tag{4.6}$$

In order to estimate the confidence interval of that sample mean the variance has to be fist calculated. If the observations are independent of each other then the variance is calculated as follows:

$$\delta^2 = \frac{1}{N-1} \sum_{i=1}^{N} (x_i - \bar{x})^2 \tag{4.7}$$

Now, the confidence interval at a confidence level of $100(1-\alpha)\%$ is:

$$(\bar{x} - Z_{\alpha/2} \cdot \frac{\delta}{\sqrt{N}}, \bar{x} + Z_{\alpha/2} \cdot \frac{\delta}{\sqrt{N}})$$

where, $\bar{x}$ is the sample mean, $Z_{\alpha/2}$ is the upper $\alpha/2$ critical value of the standard normal distribution (can be obtained from the standard distribution table [Sta12]), δ^2 is the variance and N is the number of samples.

The *confidence* (i.e., 100(1-α)%) can take several values e.g., 99%, 95% and 90%. If the number of samples taken for calculating the confidence interval is smaller than 30 then the student-t distribution table is used as follows:

$$(\bar{x} - t_{(\alpha/2,N-1)} \cdot \frac{\delta}{\sqrt{N}}, \bar{x} + t_{(\alpha/2,N-1)} \cdot \frac{\delta}{\sqrt{N}})$$

where, $t_{(\alpha/2,N-1)}$ is the upper critical value of the t-distribution with N-1 degrees of freedom. This can be obtained from the t-distribution table [Sta12].

4.5.2 Independent Replications Method

Normally in simulations the data gathered for the statistical evaluation are correlated with each other. Thus, the confidence interval calculation method explained earlier cannot be used directly. In literature, a number of solutions exist to solve the correlated data problem: e.g., replications method, estimation of autocorrelation function, batch means and regenerative method. Within this subsection, the independent replications method is explained which is also used to evaluate the confidence interval for this thesis.

The independent replication method [Per09], as the name suggests, relies on replicating several independent simulation runs. For example, N number of replications are done each with M number of data elements:

Replication 1: $x_{11}, x_{12}, x_{13}...x_{1M}$
Replication 2: $x_{21}, x_{22}, x_{23}...x_{2M}$
Replication 3: $x_{31}, x_{32}, x_{33}...x_{3M}$
.
.
.
Replication n: $x_{N1}, x_{N2}, x_{N3}...x_{NM}$

The sample mean of each replication i can be evaluated as:

$$\bar{x_i} = \frac{1}{M} \sum_{j=1}^{M} x_{ij} \tag{4.8}$$

This leads to having N approximately independent sample means $[\overline{x_1}, \overline{x_2}, ... \overline{x_N}]$, the sample mean and variance of them will be:

$$\overline{\overline{x}} = \frac{1}{N} \sum_{i=1}^{N} \overline{x_i} \tag{4.9}$$

$$\delta^2 = \frac{1}{N-1} \sum_{i=1}^{N} \left(\overline{x_i} - \overline{\overline{x}} \right)^2 \tag{4.10}$$

Now, using this variance the confidence interval can be calculated as explained before. Although the independent replications method is easy and simple two issues still need to be determined: first, how long each independent replication should be run (i.e., choosing M which should be a large number), and the seed used for each independent run must be chosen very carefully in order to have the replications independent. The independence between the replications can be checked by calculating the autocorrelation between them.

5 LTE Virtualization

This chapter presents the concepts of network virtualization, focusing specifically on wireless virtualization of the LTE mobile communication system. A novel wireless virtualization framework is proposed and developed by this thesis, which allows mobile network operators to share the wireless spectrum as well as the infrastructure (i.e., hardware equipments). The work presented in this chapter targets proving the concept of using virtualization in wireless systems and highlighting its potential gain. The chapter is structured in the following manner: in section 5.1 the virtualization history and concepts are discussed. Section 5.2.1 describes the 4WARD European project and its virtualization architecture, the work was done by the author as part of the 4WARD project. In section 5.3 the novel LTE virtualization framework is proposed, explaining the technical details behind the framework. Proof of concept evaluations are discussed in section 5.4, where three different scenarios are presented each showing a different potential gain area within the LTE virtualization. Finally section 5.5 summarizes and concludes this chapter. The proposed LTE virtualization framework, results/achievements and other related virtualization work are published in [ZZGTG10a], [ZZGTG10b], [ZZGTG11], [ZKZG11], [KZ11], [ZLZ$^+$11], [LZZ$^+$12] and [UZZ$^+$10].

5.1 Virtualization

Virtualization is the process of creating virtual versions of physical resources that emulate the same physical characteristics. It is often used in the Information Technology (IT) context to partition a physical resource into several virtual ones, for example, virtual memory, hard disk partition and virtual machine. The virtualization concept [Sin04] was first introduced at the beginning of the 1960s, when Christopher Strachey published a paper entitled "Time Sharing in Large Fast Computers" that focused on multi-programming. Then came the IBM M44/44X Project in the mid 1960s, where the term Virtual Machine (VM) was introduced for the first time. The creation and maintenance of such virtual machines is what is known today as "Server Virtualization". The idea at that time was to create several virtual machines out of one mainframe computer to enable multi-tasking, i.e., running simultaneous applications and processes in one computer, since such computers were very expensive at the time. The virtualization concept can be applied in different areas. But from what can be seen in today's IT interest three main areas emerge that adopt the use of virtualization, and these are:

- Storage Virtualization: according to IBM [IBM03], *"it is considered as an intelligent "layer" or abstraction that pools storage from multiple storage devices into a common storage pool. Often part of a Storage Area Network (SAN)* virtualized storage appears as one device to the server-operating systems and can be centrally managed and provisioned from a single view".

- Server Virtualization: is the process of hiding the resources of the physical server and dividing the server into a number of virtual servers that share the physical resources and appear to the operating system running on top as an actual hardware. Server virtualization is used to minimize the IT cost in enterprises, as well as utilizing the full potentials of the physical servers.

- Network Virtualization: is the process of aggregating the created virtual resources into forming a Virtual Network (VNet). It enables multiple virtual networks to coexist on a common infrastructure in an isolated way. Each virtual network is operating similar to a normal network and does not necessarily have the awareness of the underlying virtualization process.

5.1.1 Server Virtualization

Within this section, the server virtualization area is discussed in detail since it is closely related to the main work of this chapter. It is the virtualization of servers by hiding the underlying physical resources and dividing them between several newly created virtual instances. For the server users it appears like several physical servers each with its own operating system, and they are not aware of the virtualization process. The server administrator uses special software to create these isolated virtual instances. There are three different ways used to virtualize a server: full virtualization, para virtualization and operating system virtualization (OS virtualization).

Full virtualization: It uses the guest/host approach. It requires a special software layer that sits on top of the physical hardware and interacts with the machine physical resources. This layer is often called "Hypervisor", or sometimes it is also known as "Virtual Machine Monitor (VMM)". The hypervisor provides the necessary platform for the guest VMs to operate on top. Figure 5.1 shows the full virtualization environment. The guest VMs can run an unmodified operating system (OS) and the hypervisor can create several guest VMs each running a different OS (e.g., Linux and Windows). The VMs are isolated and not aware of each other. Both VMware [VMw] and Microsoft Virtual Server [Mic] are based on the full virtualization model.

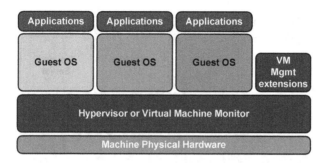

Figure 5.1: Full virtualization environment [Cha09]

Para virtualization: It uses the guest/host approach. A hypervisor is also used, but it additionally modifies the guest OS to support hyper calls over native functions. This means that the VMs runs as modified guest OS. In this technique the VMs are aware of one another. XEN [WG07] and User Mode Linux (UML), [UML] are good examples for para virtualization. Figure 5.2 shows the Para-virtualization environment.

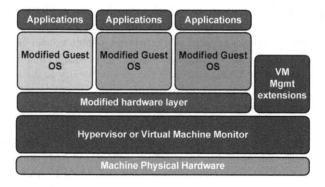

Figure 5.2: Para virtualization environment [Cha09]

OS virtualization: Unlike the previous two techniques, the OS virtualization is not based on the guest/host model. No hypervisor is used in this case, instead, the virtualization functionalities are supported within the host OS. The guest servers must use the same OS as the host which is viewed as a drawback of this approach. Figure 5.3 shows the OS virtualization environment.

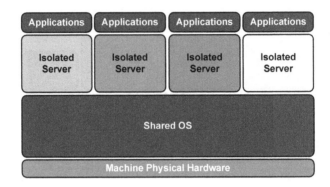

Figure 5.3: OS virtualization environment [Cha09]

5.1.2 Network Virtualization

Network virtualization is the process of combining different -virtual- network resources into a Virtual Network (VNet). The network virtualization definition was described earlier in section 5.1. Individual virtual networks can contain operator-specific protocols and architectures, which could be totally different from other co-existing virtual networks. That is why interoperability among the different network architectures becomes a crucial issue. In order to interconnect the isolated islands of virtual networks the *Folding Points* [ZZJ⁺09] concept can provide secure connections between the VNets enforcing the operator policy at the border of the VNets, as well as ensuring the proper translation of the architectures/protocols. In addition, network virtualization also provides full administrative end-to-end control for the operators over their VNets.

Many research activities, focusing on the Future Internet architecture, have been launched around the world, for example, 4WARD [4WAf] in Europe, VINI [BFH⁺06] and GENI [GEN] in the United States and AKARI [AKA10] and Asi-aFI [Asi] in Asia. By observing these projects, one tendency can be observed that network virtualization is an attractive technique which receives more and more research attention, and it will be a key area in the future network development for both testbed developments and operational networks.

VINI is a virtual network infrastructure based on PlanetLab [PMRK06], on which researchers can deploy, run and test their own protocols and services on a large scale. GENI (Global Environment for Network Innovations) is a novel suite of architectures which support a range of experimental protocols, and virtualization is one of the most important features. The AKARI Architecture Design Project aims at implementing the basic technology of a new generation network from a clean slate, and network virtualization has been seen as one of its principles applications. The Asia Future Internet Forum (AsiaFI) was founded to coordinate research and development on Future Internet, where network virtualization is on its main list of research topics. In spite of all the major research projects that has previously been mentioned, one very important piece of the puzzle is still missing, that is "Wireless" Virtualization. Wireless virtualization, according to the best of the author's knowledge, has not yet received the appropriate attention entitled to and only little work has been done in this field.

5.2 4WARD Project

4WARD is a large European project that started at the beginning of 2008, with 36 partners including telecommunication operators, manufacturers and research institutions. The main goal of the project is to make the development of networks and networked applications faster and easier, leading to both more advanced and more affordable communication services. The project is structured into six different paradigms: three of which focus on innovative solutions of single network architectures [4WAc] [4WAd] [4WAe], one focuses on network virtualization [4WAb] and one focuses on the architectural paradigm [4WAa] that looks into designing a framework for the Future Internet Architecture. In addition, there is one paradigm [CW08] that looks into how the paradigms fit together, as well as taking care of some non-technical issues that are of high significance, e.g., governance and regulations. Since one of the main foci in this thesis is network virtualization, the 4WARD virtualization work package is explained in more detail in the next subsection. The virtualization work explained in this thesis was done as part of the 4WARD project (mainly the virtualization work package).

5.2.1 4WARD Virtualization Paradigm

The 4WARD network virtualization technique aims at utilizing virtual networks as means to achieve the following objectives [4WAb]:

- Supporting concurrent operation of different networks over a single shared infrastructure by means of virtual networks

- Enabling a rapid deployment of new network architectures and communication protocols

- Providing inter-working facilities to allow data exchange between different VNets when desired

The idea is to use virtualization as a tool to separate the current roles of the infrastructure and service provider played by today's Internet Service Provider (ISP) into separate entities. This is done in order to open the market for new business roles and models. In addition, the possibility of instantiating virtual networks across several infrastructure providers is also foreseen; which gives the virtual network operators the necessary end-to-end control that is not possible within today's network.

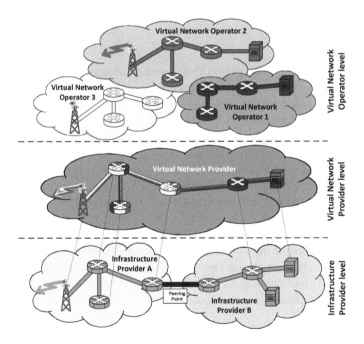

Figure 5.4: Network virtualization proposed business model

Figure 5.4 shows the different new players and business entities that are proposed by the 4WARD network virtualization paradigm. Basically the paradigm suggests three different business models:

- **Infrastructure Providers**: own and maintain the physical network devices. They need to virtualize their physical resources in order to offer them to the virtual network providers to form VNets, e.g., creating a number of virtual links from a physical link, or creating virtual nodes from a physical one.

- **Virtual Network Providers**: are brokers between the other two business roles; their main role is to receive requests from the VNet operators, negotiate and find the best suitable candidate of the virtual resources from different infrastructure providers and finally setting up the VNet.

- **Virtual Network Operators**: are responsible for running the VNet to provide services to the end users.

5.3 Wireless Virtualization in Mobile Communication

This thesis focuses on wireless network virtualization, more specifically the virtualization of mobile communication systems. Within today's daily life, mobile communications are evidently playing a big role in the way people communicate and access information. In the future, mobile communications will require large amounts of valuable wireless resources, especially when dealing with heterogeneous wireless networks, and when looking at the extremely high data rates that are set as targets for future systems. Within the scope of this thesis, the focus is on virtualization of the Long Term Evolution (LTE) network as an important use case of mobile network virtualization. Nevertheless, the proposed approach for LTE virtualization in this thesis is as well applicable for any other wireless communication systems.

Network virtualization allows operators to share the same physical infrastructure and have networks coexisting in a flexible, dynamic manner. Thus utilizing the available resources much more efficiently. This implies that the physical infrastructure needs to be virtualized into a number of virtual resources being offered to the different virtual networks. In consequence, resource virtualization requires all entities to be virtualized: routers, servers, links (wired or wireless) and host/end systems. The virtualization of servers, routers and wired links has been extensively studied in the literature [Cis] [VMw] [VRO] [KMC$^+$00] [BMM$^+$08] and [WG07]. However, the wireless part has not yet received major consideration within today's research community. Some early studies have already started, for example, in [SB08] a generic framework of wireless virtualization is proposed, and in [MBH+08] a space versus time separation for IEEE 802.11 WLAN wireless virtualization is studied.

Virtualization of wireless resources on the air interface is basically a scheduling problem of Transmitter/Receiver power, frequency, time and code or space allocation. It is very similar to the well known wireless multiple access schemes: FDMA, TDMA, CDMA and SDMA (Figure 5.5), in which the transmission of the different virtual networks can be allocated on the different dimensions of the wireless resources.

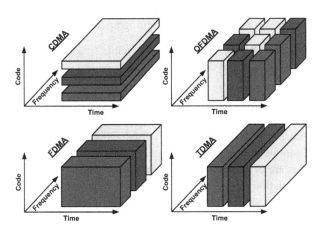

Figure 5.5: Multiple access schemes

Virtualization of wireless resources for mobile communication is a complex challenge. First, the wireless resources have to be shared and assigned (e.g., at the Base Station) to different Virtual Network Operators (VNOs). The sharing needs to be fair. Fairness in wireless systems can be defined differently: fairness in terms of spectrum used, or power used, or a product of these two, or even fairness of QoS delivered to the end users. Furthermore, it is not sufficient to look only at the resources that are being shared, assigned or scheduled at one base station, but also the interference caused by sharing these resources need to be considered. This is even more complex as neighboring base stations of different (virtual) network operators could use completely different transmission technologies.

5.3.1 Motivation behind Mobile Network Virtualization

Mobile networks are one of the fastest growing technologies that are influencing major aspects of the way we communicate and access information. The virtualization of mobile networks is a subset of the wireless virtualization. Virtualizing mobile networks and sharing their resources will bring a more efficient utilization of the scarce wireless resources. Furthermore, network virtualization can reduce the amount necessary base station equipment and thus reduce the required energy to run wireless networks, as well as reducing the overall investment capital required by mobile operators to setup their own infrastructure.

Network virtualization also enables completely new value chains. Small players can come into the market and provide new services to their customers using a virtual network [ZKZG11] [KZ11]. This also allows completely new future networks, e.g., isolating one virtual network (like a banking network) from a best effort Internet access network. Sharing the physical resources will enable these new small players to enter the market and provide their services wherever required. Furthermore, the idea of being able to share the frequency resources among multiple operators is very appealing. This gives operators the flexibility to expand or shrink their networks and the air interface resources they use. This will lead to more efficient overall resource utilization and reduced energy consumption.

5.3.2 LTE Virtualization Framework

The future of mobile communication is all about heterogeneous networks and being able to share the different wireless resources so that users can move between different networks seamlessly without any interruptions. Virtualization of the mobile communication system is seen as a fundamental step to achieve this goal. This of course means that the mobile communication system has to be virtualized, so that the operators will obtain the required flexibility in order to achieve their individual desired targets. LTE is the next generation of mobile communication. In this thesis, it is chosen as a case study to demonstrate how network virtualization is applied in mobile networks and what benefits can be achieved.

Virtualizing the LTE network means that the infrastructure of the LTE system (including eNodeBs, routers, Ethernet links ...) has to be virtualized. This is done so that multiple mobile network operators can create their own virtual networks depending on their individual requirements and goals, while using a common infrastructure. The main technical challenges faced are how to virtualize the physical infrastructure to support such scenarios and what kind of architectural changes are required in the current LTE system. Two different categories of the virtualization processes are mainly foreseen, these are:

1. Physical infrastructure virtualization: the infrastructure of the LTE network (i.e., nodes and links) has to be virtualized so that different virtual mobile operators can create their own network.

2. Air interface virtualization: being able to virtualize the LTE spectrum, i.e., the physical spectrum resources can be shared by different virtual mobile operators.

The latter case is the focus of this work, because the first part can be broken down into node (routers and servers) as well as link virtualization, which have been extensively studied in the literature as mentioned before; while virtualizing the air interface of the LTE system is a completely new concept. There has been some similar work done in terms of spectrum sharing especially when considering Software Defined Radio (SDR) [DMA03], but this was only done for the unlicensed bands, and not for whole systems using licensed bands such as LTE.

5.3.2.1 Framework Architecture

Virtualizing the LTE air interface also implies that the eNodeB has to be virtualized, since it is the entity that is responsible for accessing the radio channel and scheduling the air interface resources. Virtualizing the eNodeB is similar to node virtualization. In node virtualization, there are a number of solutions where the physical resources of the virtual machine (like the CPU cycles, memory, I/O devices etc.) are being shared between multiple virtual instances of virtual operating systems. XEN [WG07] for example is a well known PC virtualization solution that calls the entity which is responsible for scheduling the physical resources a "Hypervisor".

Within this thesis, an LTE virtualization framework is proposed [ZZGTG11] following a similar principle to the XEN virtualization. A hypervisor layer is added on top of the physical resources of the LTE eNodeB, which is responsible for virtualizing the eNodeB node, as well as the spectrum. The framework architecture can be seen in Figure 5.6.

The architecture shows that the physical LTE eNodeB has been virtualized into a number of virtual eNodeBs, assuming that each will be used by a different operator. The physical resources are being scheduled among the different virtual instances via the hypervisor (similar to XEN). In addition, the LTE hypervisor is also responsible for scheduling the air interface resources (that is the OFDMA

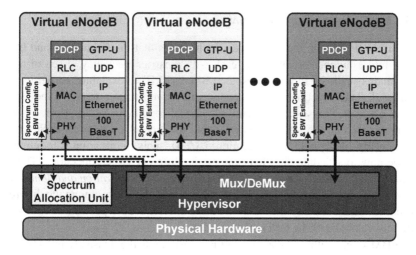

Figure 5.6: LTE virtualization framework architecture

sub-carriers) between the different virtual eNodeBs. In this work, only the latter functionality of the hypervisor is focused on, that is the air interface scheduling. For the first part, similar solutions already exists, for example, VANU MultiRAN [VAN] which is a solution used to support multiple virtual base stations all running on a single hardware platform. Thus, the multiple virtual base stations can share the antennas, hardware platform and the backhaul. MultiRAN also allows multiple operators to virtually share a single physical network.

In this framework architecture two new entities will be highlighted. The first entity is the *"Spectrum Configuration and Bandwidth Estimation"*, this is responsible for configuring the spectrum which the virtual eNodeB is operating in. It is also responsible for estimating the required spectrum each operator requires over time. This estimated spectrum is then fed back to the hypervisor; the reason why this is needed by the hypervisor will be explained later in section 5.3.2.4. The second entity is the *"Spectrum Allocation Unit"*, it is responsible for scheduling the spectrum among the different virtual eNodeBs based on the information gathered from different virtual eNodeBs, e.g., the spectrum estimated.

5.3.2.2 LTE Hypervisor Algorithm

LTE uses OFDMA in the downlink, which means that the frequency band is divided into a number of sub-bands each with a carrier frequency. Each of these sub-bands is called a Physical Resource Block (PRB) as explained earlier in section 3.4.3. The Hypervisor continuously collects information from the individual virtual eNodeB stacks, such as their user channel conditions, loads, priorities, QoS requirements, and the information related to the type of the contract each virtual operator has (described later in section 5.3.2.4). This information is required to decide how to schedule the PRBs among the different virtual operators. The information collection is carried out by the *"Spectrum Configuration and Bandwidth Estimation"* unit in the virtual eNodeB. Scheduling the PRBs among the different virtual eNodeBs actually means distributing the frequency spectrum between the different eNodeBs of the different operators.

OFDMA scheduling is not new and has been studied extensively in [ABJS06] [AMVC07] [EK06] and [EKW08], However, what is new is that the frequency spectrum has to be firstly scheduled among the different virtual operators and then each virtual operator will schedule its allocated spectrum among its users. This means that there are two layers of scheduling: one layer for splitting the spectrum between the different virtual operators, and one layer for splitting the allocated spectrum among the users belonging to the same operator. The first one is even more challenging due to the additional degree of freedom that has been added to the scheduling. The scheduling can be based on different criteria such as: bandwidth, data rate, power, interference, pre-defined contract, channel condition, traffic load or a combination of these. What is important at the end is that the hypervisor has to convert these criteria into a number of PRBs to be scheduled to each operator. The main technical challenge in this work is how to make sure that the PRB allocation is fair, and at the same time the allocated PRBs can still enable the operators to satisfy their own as well as their users' requirements.

5.3.2.3 Operator Bandwidth Estimation

In order for the virtualization framework to work a feedback mechanism is required so that the hypervisor is able to know the actual demand of each of the virtual operators. This is then used to decide how to distribute the spectrum between the different virtual operators. Each operator sends a proper estimation of how much bandwidth (i.e., resources) it needs. This estimate is fed-back to the hypervisor's spectrum allocation unit from each of the virtual eNodeB instances running on top of the hypervisor. The correct estimation is a crucial part because underestimating the required bandwidth may lead to not having sufficient allocated spectrum for the virtual operator, which will in turn influence the performance of that operator's users. On the other hand, overestimating the required spectrum will lead to wasting resources.

The bandwidth estimation is calculated for each operator, and since it is an estimation of the operator's required spectrum it has to be calculated over some period of time. The instantaneous bandwidth required by each operator can be calculated each TTI, thus the estimation entity will collect a number of instantaneous bandwidth values over the defined estimation time interval. These values need to be converted into a single one that can be sent back to the allocation unit as an indication of the required bandwidth over that time interval. The most straightforward approach is to take the simple average value of the instantaneous bandwidth. However, simple average values may not be relied on as they may give wrong indications especially if it has some spikes (that is onetime events with high values) within the data. In order to avoid these single time events, and filter those out, it is proposed to use the Exponential Moving Average (EMA) [HUN86]. The EMA gives more weight to recent values while not discarding older values. This makes it a perfect solution for the bandwidth estimation, because the most recent values are the up-to-date values of the operator bandwidth requirement. Thus, the bandwidth estimation is calculated as follows:

$$E(N) = \alpha \times E(N-1) + (1 - \alpha) \times PRBsTTI(N) \qquad (5.1)$$

Here, $E(N)$ represents the moving average of the required PRBs (estimate of the required bandwidth), N is a TTI instance within the hypervisor decision interval and α is the smoothing factor indicating the weighting between 0 and 1. *PRB-sTTI(N)* is the instantaneous PRB count at the Nth TTI, calculated by summing the PRBs that were additionally needed to schedule the un-served users within this TTI minus the number of left PRBs that were not used. *E(N)* can take both positive and negative values, as the operator would either need more PRBs or would like to give some PRBs back that are not required.

5.3.2.4 Contract-Based Framework

In this section, a practical framework for LTE virtualization and spectrum sharing is proposed to share the LTE spectrum among different virtual operators (each with different goals and requirements). The framework [ZZGTG10b] is based on offering different contracts that each operator can chose from the infrastructure provider. Based on the requirements of each virtual operator a suitable contract can be made to express these requirements and satisfy them. In this framework, four different contract types are defined and offered by the infrastructure provider to the virtual operators and these are:

a. Fixed guarantees: the operator requests a fixed bandwidth that will be allocated to it at all times whether it is used or not.

b. Dynamic guarantees: the operator gets the bandwidth (in terms of number of PRBs) according to its actual need. The bandwidth is upper bounded by a maximum value that is specified by the contract. If the operator requires the maximum bandwidth, the infrastructure provider will allocate it to him; otherwise only the required bandwidth is allocated, which can be less than the maximum value. The operator only pays for the actual used bandwidth and thus can save cost.

c. Best effort (BE) with minimum guarantees: the operator specifies a minimum guaranteed bandwidth which will be allocated at all times [1]. The minimum bandwidth is always guaranteed and the additional part is added in a BE manner.

d. Best effort with no guarantees: the operator does not specify any guarantees for its traffic and the operator is assigned any bandwidth that is remaining, i.e., in a pure BE manner.

The hypervisor uses the estimation value (calculated according to equation 5.1) to allocate each virtual operator's spectrum. This is used specifically for contract types b, c and d. For contract type b, this would serve as the actual allocated bandwidth for that operator, upper bounded by the contract maximum value. For the BE contracts (contract c and d) the hypervisor will first allocate the operators of contract c with their minimum guaranteed value and whatever PRBs left at the end would be distributed between the BE operators. The split is based on a fairness factor that is calculated as follows:

$$F_i = E_i(N) / E_{total} \qquad (5.2)$$

where F_i is the fairness factor of operator i, $E_i(N)$ is the PRB estimate of operator i, and the E_{total} is the total best effort PRB estimate over all best effort operators (e.g., K number of BE operators), and is calculated as follows:

$$E_{total} = \sum_{i=1}^{K} E_i(N) \qquad (5.3)$$

---

[1]Conceptually a maximum value may also be configured for that contract acting as an upper bound for the operator allocated bandwidth.

The number of PRBs allocated for each BE virtual operator is calculated as follows:

$$PRBsAlloc_i = int\,(F_i \times LeftPRBs) \qquad (5.4)$$

where *int* is the integer function, and the LeftPRBs is the number of PRBs left for the BE operators after allocating the guaranteed operators.

The proposed framework for the contract-based algorithm in the hypervisor is shown in Figure 5.7.

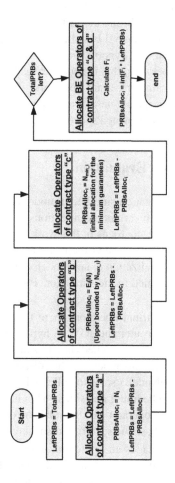

Figure 5.7: The general hypervisor algorithm framework

The framework starts by allocating spectrum to the operators with guaranteed contracts. First of all, operators with contract type a, or the fixed contract operators, are allocated their spectrum (in terms of number of PRBs, i.e., $PRBsAlloc_i$) based on the amount specified by their contract (N_i). The TotalPRBs represents the total amount of PRBs that an infrastructure provider owns which is the total owned spectrum/bandwidth. After allocating all the operators of contract type a, the hypervisor starts allocating operators with contract type b. These operators are allocated their spectrum based on their bandwidth estimation upper bounded by the contract maximum value. After that the hypervisor starts allocating the BE operators by first allocating operators with contract type c with their minimum guaranteed spectrum and then splitting the rest of the left spectrum between them and the operators with contract type d based on the mechanism explained earlier in equation 5.2. In addition, the hypervisor needs to provide admission control in accepting new virtual operators, this is necessary as the infrastructure provider has to guarantee the spectrum for certain operators. This means that the infrastructure provider will not accept any new virtual operator request if the sum of the guaranteed spectrum exceeds its owned spectrum.

5.4 LTE Virtualization Evaluation

In this work, the LTE virtualization simulation model is built based on the developed OPNET LTE model with certain modifications to include the virtualization process. As mentioned earlier, the focus of this work is not on the node/link virtualization but rather on the air interface virtualization (i.e., spectrum sharing). Due to this reason, node/link virtualization is not modeled, instead a perfect node/link virtualization process is assumed in the simulator. Figure 5.8 shows the LTE virtualization simulation model.

It can be seen that three virtual operators share the same infrastructure, each with its own virtual eNodeB, router and aGW. A hypervisor entity can also be noticed, which has the responsibility of scheduling the air interface resources among the different virtual eNodeBs. The hypervisor has direct access to the MAC layers of each of the LTE virtual eNodeBs so as to collect all the required relevant information to be used for the scheduling decisions. This information can consist of, e.g., user channel conditions, operator's traffic load and operator's contracts which is used by the hypervisor to base the spectrum distribution decision on.

In order to find the advantages and potential gains of the LTE virtualization, three different scenarios are investigated in this chapter. The scenarios exploit the multiplexing gain as well as the multi-user diversity gain, which are compared with

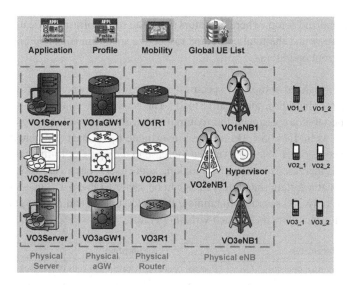

Figure 5.8: LTE virtualization simulation model in OPNET

a non-virtualized LTE system with the same configuration. The non-virtualized LTE system represents the current setup of the LTE system. The scenarios and their respective results are presented in the next subsections.

5.4.1 Multiplexing Gain-Based Analysis

This scenario exploits the multiplexing gain that can be achieved through the LTE virtualization and the spectrum sharing [ZZGTG10a]. Normally, the radio access network is dimensioned with an overbooked frequency band in order to handle the worst case scenarios when the operators experience their peak traffic loads (e.g., in busy hours). If the different mobile operators experience their peak loads at different times, or if the instantaneous peaks within each virtual operator busy hour occurs at slightly shifted times (i.e., not exactly at the same time) then a potential multiplexing gain can be achieved through spectrum sharing among the different mobile operators. This will lead to a better resource utilization. This simulation scenario compares two different setups:

- Legacy setup: which is today's mobile network setup, where each operator owns a frequency band and is not sharing this band with any other operators.

- Virtualized setup: where operators share the same infrastructure using virtualization and the total combined respective spectrum is shared between the different operators.

In the virtualized setup, the spectrum is scheduled between the different virtual operators based on their traffic load. The scenario is configured so that the virtual operators are assigned the required spectrum to serve their users, and are configured as in Table 5.1. In order to investigate the impact and benefits of the air interface resource sharing a sudden increase in the operator traffic load is introduced. This increase is emulated, by making some users start a video conferencing application at a certain time interval, as can be seen in Table 5.1. The video traffic is used for only 300 seconds, to emulate the sudden peak, and is configured to be at different time intervals for each virtual operator.

Parameter	Assumption
Number of virtual operators	3 virtual operators with circular cells of 375 meters radius
Total Number of PRBs (Spectrum)	75 PRBs (15 MHz), each operator has 25 PRBs
Mobility model	Random Way Point (RWP) with vehicular speed (120km/h)
Number of users per VO	20 VoIP users and 20 Video users
MAC priority mapping	VoIP traffic is mapped to MAC-QoS-Class 1
	Video traffic is mapped to MAC-QoS-Class 5
Channel model	described in section 4.3.5
VoIP traffic model	Silence/Talk Spurt length = negative exponential distribution with 3 seconds mean
	Encoder Scheme: GSM EFR
	Continuous call throughout the whole simulation time
Video traffic model	24 Frames per second with frame size: 1562 bytes
	Duration: 300 seconds
	Starting time: VO1 = 100s, VO2 = 400s, VO3 = 700s
Hypervisor resolution	1 second (for the virtualized setup)
Simulation run time	1000 seconds
Number of Simulation seeds	20 seeds; simulations with 95% confidence interval

Table 5.1: Scenario I simulation configurations

Figure 5.9 shows the bandwidth in MHz representing the total number of PRBs assigned by the hypervisor to each virtual operator. It can be noticed that the allocated bandwidth changes with time corresponding to the variation of the traffic load of each operator. In the time interval between 100 - 400 seconds, it can be seen that operator 1 has been allocated a much higher bandwidth compared to the other two operators. This is due to the scenario configuration, where operator 1 has 20 additional video users that are active during this time period and thus cause an increase in the traffic load. Similarly, there is a traffic load increase in the time interval between 400 - 700 seconds for VO2 and between 700 - 1000 seconds for VO3. The result also shows that during the peak traffic situation the operator can get more than 5 MHz (25 PRBs) by sharing the free spectrum of the other two operators, and this would not be possible in without the virtualization process.

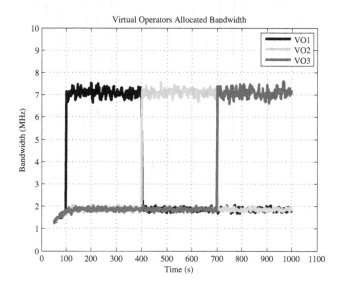

Figure 5.9: Virtual operators allocated bandwidth over simulation time

Figure 5.10 and Figure 5.11 show the VoIP user air interface throughput in kbps (i.e., throughput between the eNodeB and UE physical layers) and the application end-to-end delay in ms respectively. It can be seen that the VoIP users have similar performance in both setups (virtualized and legacy) since the VoIP traffic is put on a higher MAC priority class. The MAC scheduler first serves the VoIP users before serving the video users. In general, the VoIP users require a smaller amount of resources due to their low traffic demand, and the 25 PRBs configured for the legacy setup are far more than enough to serve the 20 VoIP users in this example.

Figure 5.11 shows that the virtualization setup suffers from a slightly higher delay values because in some cases when the channel conditions experienced by certain users are bad the scheduler assigns more PRBs to those users in order to overcome the bad channel conditions. For the legacy setup, enough free resources exist that can be allocated, whereas in the virtualized setup there are no free re-

sources since the allocated number of PRBs is based on the average amount of
PRBs required by the operator and this causes the slightly increased delay.

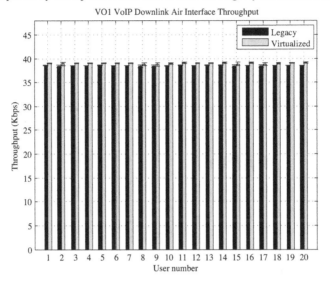

Figure 5.10: Virtual operator 1 VoIP air interface throughput

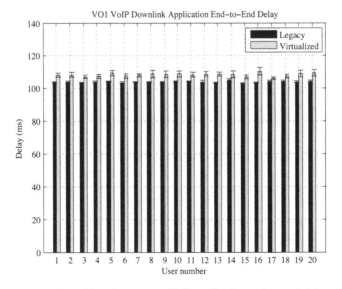

Figure 5.11: Virtual operator 1 VoIP application end-to-end delay

Figure 5.12 shows the video users' application end-to-end delay. The results show that the video users have much better performance in the virtualized setup compared to the legacy setup. This is because in the legacy setup the 25 configured PRBs are not enough to serve all 20 video users in each TTI. As a result, only a few number of the video users are served in each TTI. Since the MAC scheduler has a proportional fair characteristic all of the video users can be served at the end. But the video user traffic needs to be buffered longer, hence, increasing the video end-to-end delay. However, for the virtualized setup the virtual operator is able to use the free resources from the other virtual operators. This means that the air interface resources can be higher than the 25 PRBs when required and this will be enough to serve all of the video users without causing any additional buffering delays. The results of the other two virtual operators are similar to VO1 results and thus are not shown.

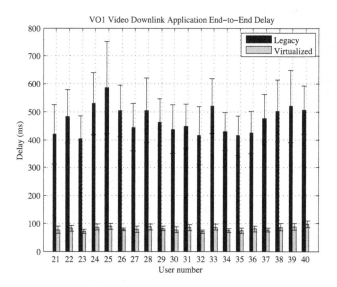

Figure 5.12: Virtual operator 1 video application end-to-end delay

5.4.2 Multi-User Diversity Gain-Based Analysis

This scenario investigates the multi-user diversity gain that can be obtained by applying LTE air interface virtualization and spectrum sharing. Since OFDMA is used the user channels are normally frequency selective, which means that each user will be experiencing different channel conditions on different PRBs. Therefore the multi-user diversity can be exploited where the channel-aware scheduler assigns the PRBS to the users experiencing better channel conditions. Virtualization enables the VOs to share their individual spectrum, which also means that the scheduler of each virtual operator has a bigger set of PRBs to exploit the multi-user diversity, which can bring additional multi-user diversity gain to the system.

This scenario shows that even in the case where no multiplexing is allowed between the different virtual operators, and each operator still has a fixed amount of spectrum, a gain can still be achieved if the spectrum is dynamically chosen based on the user channel conditions [ZZGTG11]. In this scenario two different setups are compared against each other as follows:

• Legacy setup: which is similar to today's mobile network setup where each operator owns a fixed amount of spectrum that is pre-allocated throughout the whole simulation.

• Virtualized setup: which aims at showing how the multi-user diversity gain can be achieved by sharing the spectrum among the operators, with the total amount of spectrum each operator gets is fixed and not changing (no multiplexing).

The rest of the simulation configurations is given in Table 5.2.

Parameter	Assumption
Number of virtual operators	3 virtual operators with circular cells of 375 meters radius
Total Number of PRBs	- 75 PRBs or 15 MHz (5MHz for each operator)
	- 150 PRBs or 30 MHz (10MHz for each operator)
	- 300 PRBs or 60 MHz (20MHz for each operator)
Mobility model	Random Way Point (RWP) with vehicular speed (120 km/h)
Number of users	VO1: 1, 2, 3, 4, 5, 10, 15 FTP users
	VO2: 1, 2, 3, 4, 5, 10, 15 FTP users
	VO3: 1, 2, 3, 4, 5, 10, 15 FTP users
Channel model	described in section 4.3.5
MAC layer scheduler	Max-C/I ^{2}
DL traffic model	FTP traffic with full buffer occupancy
	File size = 5 MByte, next file is loaded immediately
	when previous file finishes
Hypervisor resolution	1 second (for the virtualized setup)
Simulation run time	1000 seconds

Table 5.2: Scenario II simulation configurations

Figure 5.13 shows the average cell throughput of virtual operator 1. The cell throughput is shown against various number of users (from 1 user all the way up to 15 users), as well as different system bandwidth (i.e., 5, 10 and 20 MHz). There are several findings from these results. First of all, the virtual setup achieves higher average cell throughput compared to the legacy setup, as a result of higher multi-user diversity by applying virtualization. This additional multi-user diversity gain is obtained due to the fact that the virtual operator can choose which PRBs to use in order to schedule the users from a larger spectrum selection (3 times larger).

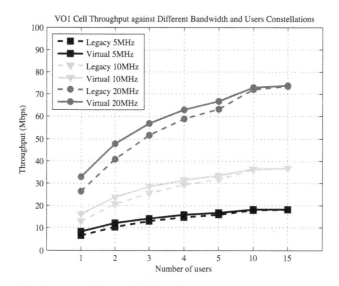

Figure 5.13: Virtual operator 1 cell throughput with and without virtualization

It can also be noticed that the gap between the virtual scenario and the legacy one decreases when the number of users is increased. The reason for that is the fact that when the number of users increases, the achieved multi-user diversity gain in the legacy scenario is nearly fully exploited (converging towards the maximum gain) since the probability of finding a user with good channel condition on each PRB increases. The absolute gain in cell throughput can be more clearly seen in figure 5.14. This is the difference in cell throughput between the virtual and the legacy scenario. It can be observed that the gain in cell throughput decreases when the number of users increases. Furthermore, it is found that when the overall

---

[2]The max-C/I algorithm schedules the user with the highest instantaneous SINR value so as to max-imize the system throughput. It is often a very unfair scheduler since users with bad channel conditions might starve.

spectrum is increased the gain in cell throughput increases as well. This is because that with more spectrum resources the probability of finding a PRB where the user is experiencing good channel conditions is much higher due to the larger spectrum selection. It needs to be noted that in case of one user there is no multi-user diversity gain at all, and thus the absolute gain increases from one user to two users, and then gradually goes down with more users. The results of the other two virtual operators are not shown due to their similarity to operator 1.

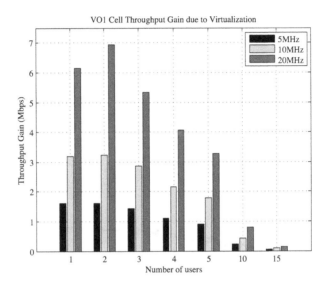

Figure 5.14: Virtual operator 1 cell throughput gain due to virtualization

The presented results demonstrate that with the air interface virtualization and spectrum sharing, even though each operator uses a fixed amount of spectrum (no multiplexing), but being able to choose the suitable PRB from a larger spectrum selection for the users can lead to a higher cell throughput. That means applying LTE air interface virtualization and spectrum sharing improves the multi-user diversity gain, since the chance of finding the best PRBs for each user according to his channel condition increases compared to the legacy scenario.

5.4.3 Contract-Based Framework Analysis

In this scenario the contract based framework explained earlier in 5.3.2.4 is evaluated. Two different simulation setups are compared against each other in order to highlight the benefits of the framework. The simulation configurations can be found in Table 5.3. The evaluated simulation scenarios are:

- Legacy setup: which is today's mobile network setup, where each operator owns a frequency band and is not sharing this band with any other operator.

- Virtualized setup: where operators are sharing the same infrastructure using virtualization and the total combined respective spectrum is shared between the different operators based on their contracts.

Parameter	Assumption
Number of virtual operators	4 virtual operators with circular cells of 375 meters radius
Total Number of PRBs	75 PRBs (15 MHz)
Legacy scenario	each of VO1, VO2 and VO3 has 25 PRBs
Virtualized scenario	VO1 - VO4 shares the 75 PRBs based on their contracts
Mobility model	Random Way Point (RWP) with vehicular speed (120 km/h)
Number of users	VO1: 15 Video users each with 300 Kbps rate
	VO2: 15 Video users each with 128 Kbps rate
	VO3: 20 Video users each with 300 Kbps rate and 5 FTP users
	VO4: 9 VoIP users
Contracts Configuration	VO1: Guaranteed contract with fixed 25 PRBs
	VO2: Dynamic guaranteed contract with max value of 25 PRBs
	VO3: Best effort with min guarantees contract, with a minimum of 15 PRBs
	VO4: Best effort with no guarantees contract
Channel model	described in section 4.3.5
VoIP traffic model	Silence/Talk Spurt length = negative exponential distribution with 3 seconds mean
	Encoder Scheme: GSM EFR
	Call Duration: Uniform distribution (60, 180) seconds
	Inter-Call Time: Exp (60) seconds
300 Kbps Video traffic model	24 Frames per second with frame size: 1562 bytes
	Duration: Continuous
128 Kbps Video traffic model	24 Frames per second with frame size: 666 bytes
	Duration: Exp. distribution (60) seconds
	Inter-Call Time: Poisson distribution (60) seconds
FTP traffic model	File Size: 15 Mbytes
	Inter-Request Time: Exp. distribution (60) seconds
Hypervisor resolution	1 second (for the virtualized setup)
Estimate α	0.5
Simulation run time	1000 seconds
Number of Simulation seeds	20 seeds; simulations with 95% confidence interval

Table 5.3: Scenario III simulation configurations

Figure 5.15 shows the bandwidth and the number of PRBs that each virtual operator is allocated over time.

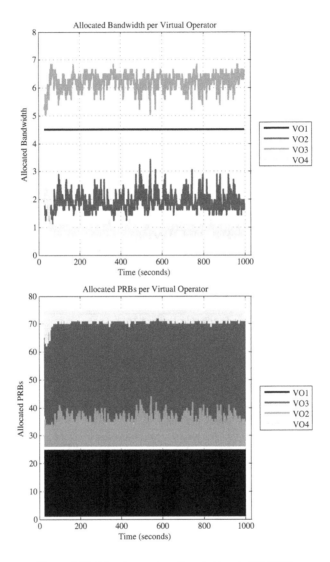

Figure 5.15: Virtual operator allocated bandwidth/PRBs

The infrastructure bandwidth is divided into a number of PRBs each occupies 180kHz. It can be noticed that for the 1st operator the PRBs allocation is fixed to 25 PRBs (from PRB number 1 till PRB number 25), since it is using the "fixed guarantees" contract. As for the other three operators, it can be seen that the allocated number of PRBs changes with time depending on the traffic load and the operator contract. It can also be seen that VO3 is using higher bandwidth than the rest of the operators mainly by sharing the free left bandwidth of VO2 with VO4.

Figure 5.16 shows VO1 video users application end-to-end delay. Similar performance can be noticed in both scenarios (with/without virtualization). This is due to the guaranteed fixed allocation contract that this VO has setup with the infrastructure operator, since the operator has the same bandwidth in both scenarios.

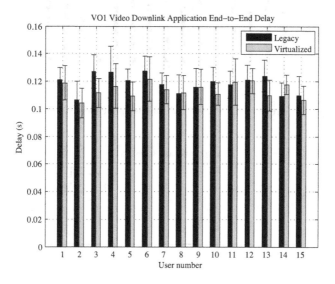

Figure 5.16: Virtual operator 1 video downlink application end-to-end delay

The average per user application end-to-end delay in VO2 is shown in Figure 5.17, a higher delay can be noticed in the virtualized setup. This is because in some time periods due the mobility the user might have bad channel conditions. The users need to use more PRBs to compensate the bad conditions and maintain the same rate over the air interface; this is not possible in the virtualization scenario (in contrast to the legacy scenario with total of 25 PRBs). This in turn increases the application end-to-end delay; nevertheless, the delay in the virtualization scenario is still within acceptable range.

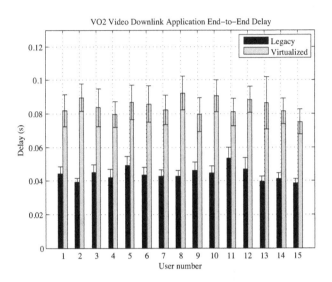

Figure 5.17: Virtual operator 2 video downlink application end-to-end delay

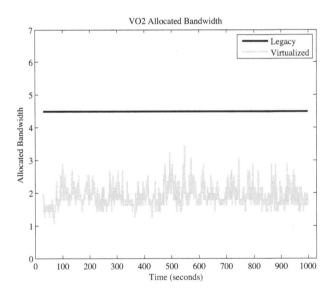

Figure 5.18: Virtual operator 2 downlink allocated bandwidth

An additional advantage for VO2 that was not so obvious in the previous results is the better air interface resource utilization as compared to the legacy scenario, which seems to be wasting the resources (Figure 5.18). This is a big advantage, because the operator will be able to cut cost down; payment will only be based on the used resources. A big difference in the end-to-end delay of VO3 video users exist, this can be seen clearly in Figure 5.19. The legacy scenario suffers from a big end-to-end delay because the static spectrum that this operator owns is not enough to serve all of the users; on the other hand, the virtualized scenario manages to have reasonable end-to-end delay since the operator can have more spectrum by taking the free ones from the other virtual operators. The operator may also enhance its performance by borrowing some of the free resources of the other operators; this obviously means better overall resource utilization which is a big advantage.

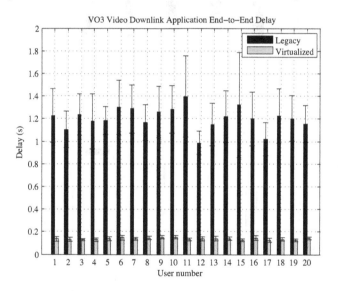

Figure 5.19: Virtual operator 3 video downlink application end-to-end delay

Figure 5.20 shows the average file download time of VO3 FTP users. The results show that the legacy scenario has more than double the download time when compared with the virtualized scenario. Again, this is because VO3 has more spectrum due to virtualization meaning that the FTP users can have more resources allocated to them and hence achieve higher throughput over the air interface. The average number of FTP file downloads is also much higher in the virtualized scenario as seen in Figure 5.21.

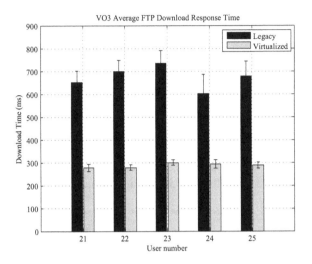

Figure 5.20: Virtual operator 3 average FTP download time

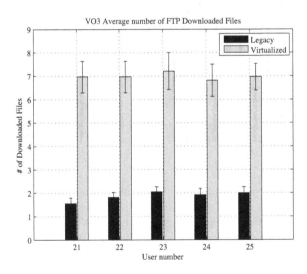

Figure 5.21: Virtual operator 3 average number of FTP Files downloaded

Finally, one more additional benefit that the virtualization may well provides is enabling small operators to serve a small number of users for specific purposes. In this particular case, the fourth virtual operator is defined within the virtualized scenario. This virtual operator is a small operator with only 9 users and is configured with a best effort and no guarantees contract. Figure 5.22 shows virtual operator 4 VoIP users end-to-end delay. The results confirm that these small operators can still coexist with other operators and support its users by taking only some of the spectrum left by other bigger virtual operators. However, it can still happen that for some time instances that there will be no free spectrum left, thus this operator will not have any spectrum to serve the users with. This is why such operators are better suited offering best effort services, where no QoS guarantees are expected by the users.

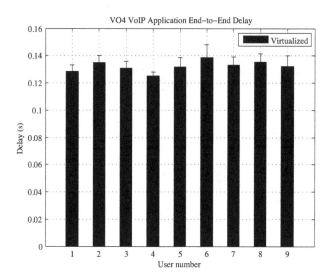

Figure 5.22: Virtual operator 4 VoIP downlink application end-to-end delay

5.5 Conclusion

This chapter introduced and discussed network virtualization as one of the new enabling tools for the future Internet/networks. The main focus of the work is wireless virtualization, specifically in mobile networks. The advantages introduced by the LTE virtualization based on spectrum sharing between different operators is studied and highlighted. An innovative wireless virtualization framework is proposed for the virtualization of LTE. However, the framework is not restricted to only LTE and is open to other similar infrastructure based wireless communication systems, e.g., WiMax. The framework was evaluated in several proof of concept scenarios aiming at showing the benefits of virtualization in the wireless domain: mainly in having better multiplexing gain due to spectrum sharing, as well as better overall system utilization due to the full exploitation of the multi-user diversity gain. In addition to the above achievements, further advantages of LTE virtualization can also be seen: for example, sharing the infrastructure of the LTE system is a considerably large gain because it leads to having less equipment and thus reduces the power consumption. It also reduces the capital investment since the operator does not need to buy the equipment but only lease virtual resources, which opens the market for small operators. Another advantage of LTE virtualization is the flexibility the virtualization brings into the operator's networks, the operator can shrink/expand and change his virtual network on the fly very easily which is one of the major advantages of network virtualization.

6 LTE Radio Scheduler

Scheduling in LTE is one of the main functions of the eNodeB. The eNodeB aims at achieving several goals regarding its scheduling functionality. First of all, the eNodeB targets cell throughput maximization, as well as being able to serve as many active users as possible. This is one of the important features that mobile network operators try to achieve, as it is related to their revenue. The second important objective is to satisfy the user by guaranteeing the QoS of their individual services. Looking at the scheduling problem within LTE, it is very easy to find that it is a complex multi-dimensional problem with conflicting targets and therefore a proper optimization and trade-off is required which can be achieved by the scheduler design.

As explained earlier, LTE uses OFDMA and SC-FDMA as the multiple access schemes, for both the downlink and uplink respectively. This means that the resources that the scheduler needs to distribute have both a time and a frequency component. The LTE radio scheduler is responsible for distributing a fixed number of PRBs (obtained from dividing the total system bandwidth) over a varying number of users/bearers in a fixed time interval, so-called for LTE, the Transmission Time Interval (TTI) which is set to 1ms. This scheduling has to be done for both the downlink and uplink direction, where the downlink is mainly constrained by the total transmission power of the eNodeB; while in contrast, the main constraint on the uplink arises from the multi-cell view of inter-cell interference [SBT09]. In LTE, a user can have in general several bearers, one for each service. For example, a user can have a phone call while browsing the web and downloading a file at the same time, which means for this example the user will have three different bearers. However, within this thesis work, the focus is only on a single bearer users, i.e., all the investigations done within this thesis are performed with only one bearer per user. That is why the terms *user* and *bearer* are used interchangingly within the thesis.

In this chapter, the LTE radio scheduler is described in detail. First of all, the general scheduling framework is introduced, followed by a state of the art survey on LTE schedulers. Then the LTE radio scheduler proposed and developed in this thesis is presented and explained in detail. The proposed scheduler is called "Optimized Service Aware Scheduler" (OSA) which is a proportional fair downlink scheduler with the motivation of providing service differentiation and guaranteeing quality of service (QoS). Finally, a detailed simulation analysis is presented, highlighting the achievements and performance gain of the proposed scheduler.

The proposed LTE downlink radio scheduler design, achievements and results are published in [ZZW$^+$11] [ZWGTG11b] [ZZW$^+$12].

6.1 LTE Dynamic Packet Scheduling

Two of the main functions of the LTE radio scheduling are the Dynamic Packet Scheduling and Link Adaptation. In the dynamic packet scheduling, the time-frequency resources (i.e., Physical Resource Block (PRB) see section 3.4.3) are distributed between the different active users and their corresponding packets are scheduled at the MAC Layer, the number of packets being scheduled depends on the Modulation and Coding Scheme (MCS) that the scheduler determines. The general packet scheduling framework is shown in Figure 6.1.

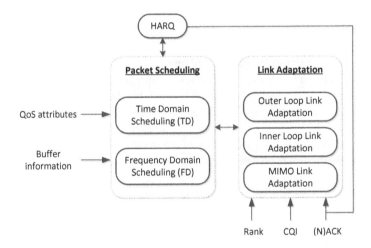

Figure 6.1: General packet scheduling framework [HT09]

As can be seen, there are a number of interactions and input parameters between the different entities. Both the HARQ manager and the link adaptation are connected to the packet scheduler, since the scheduler needs to know whether to schedule a new transmission for a certain bearer/user within this TTI, or a pending retransmission is required (as a user cannot do both at the same time). It can be seen that a number of input parameters are also required, such as: QoS attributes, buffer information and some link parameters that are fed back from the users in the uplink in the form of Channel Quality Indicator (CQI).

The packet scheduling is divided into two different stages: the first stage is the Time Domain Scheduler (TDS) and the second stage is the Frequency Domain Scheduler (FDS). The driver behind such a split is mainly simplicity. The designed scheduler has to work in real life equipment at the end of the day, where resources are limited and decisions have to be made within the one millisecond time interval. Thus, the scheduler design and implementation have to be as simple and efficient as possible. In the LTE literature such a split is recommended and is normally called decoupled time and frequency domain scheduler [KPK+08a].

6.2 LTE MAC Schedulers State of the Art

In the literature, there are many papers that deal with the problem of LTE scheduling. Many of them propose the split of the LTE scheduler into two domains: Time Domain (TD) and Frequency Domain (FD). The main reason behind the split is to reduce complexity. For example, the authors in [KPK+08a] study the effects of dynamic packet scheduling in the LTE downlink scheduler and propose the decoupled time and frequency domain packet scheduling, and use a combination of known schedulers. However, the authors also state at the end that several issues are still missing, for example, QoS differentiation between the services. In [KLZ09], it was demonstrated that the use of a proportional fair multi-user scheduler provides a superior fairness performance when the users average SINR values are fairly uniform. However, service differentiation is also not addressed.

Many publications that deal with the LTE scheduling problem combine several standard scheduling techniques for the TD and FD schedulers: e.g., Round Robin (RR), Blind Equal throughput (BET), Proportional Fair (PF), Dynamic Allocation (DA), Equal Resources (ER), Maximum Throughput (MaxT) and many others. They investigate the achievements of using the different scheduling disciplines in terms of fairness, latency reduction, spectral efficiency and system utilization. Some of these publications are [BAD08] [KPK+08b] [PMP+07] [GL08].

6.2.1 Classical Scheduling Algorithms

Scheduling in principle is a process that tries to create a trade-off, between the different system requirements mainly: fairness between users and performance maximization (e.g., cell throughput maximization). When designing a scheduling algorithm, it all depends on the balance and ratio between these requirements and what the respective operator would like to have. Two of the most famous scheduling disciplines that are on the opposite edges of the requirements metric are: Blind Equal Throughput (BET) scheduler and Maximum Throughput (MaxT) scheduler.

The BET scheduler represents the fairest algorithm, it tends to gives equal chances for every party involved (i.e., users), as well as a fair chance of the resources in order to achieve similar throughput/data rates. It also gives the users with lower accumulated throughput a higher priority than the ones with higher accumulated throughput. The priority factor calculation for the BET scheduler is as follows:

$$P_k^{BET}(t) = argmax_k \left[\frac{1}{\theta_k[t]} \right] \quad (6.1)$$

Where $P_k^{BET}(t)$ is the time domain priority factor using the BET scheduler, t is the tth TTI representing the time instance when the decision is being taken, k is the bearer number and $\overline{\theta_k[t]}$ is the normalized average throughput of bearer k ranging between 0 and 1, it is calculated as follows:

$$\overline{\theta_k[t]} = \begin{cases} (1 - 1/\tau) \times \overline{\theta_k[t-1]} + 1/\tau \times \frac{\theta_k[t]}{\theta_{max}} & \text{if bearer k is served} \\ & \text{in time slot t} \\ \\ (1 - 1/\tau) \times \overline{\theta_k[t-1]} & \text{otherwise} \end{cases} \quad (6.2)$$

where τ is the smoothing factor and is set to 1000 TTIs (1 second) in this work, $\theta_k[t]$ is the instantaneous achieved throughput at the tth TTI and θ_{max} as a normalization factor, which is defined to be the maximum throughput that can be achieved if all PRBs are used under perfect channel conditions.

The priority metric shown in equation (6.1) is calculated for all active users every TTI, and then a scheduling candidate list is created with all active users sorted based on their priorities, from the highest priorities to the lowest ones.

The BET is often viewed as the least efficient of the overall resource utilization, or the performance maximization. The explanation is rather simple, if one looks at a user with relatively bad channel conditions, such a user cannot in fact achieve a high transmission rate because of the bad conditions, now even though the accumulated throughput for that user will be small (due to the low transmission rates) the priority metric for that user will still be high. This means that although the user is in bad channel conditions the scheduler still allocates resources for that user, thus wasting valuable air interface resources.

The MaxT scheduler on the other hand tries to maximize the cell throughput and the system performance. It gives the highest priority to the users that can utilize the radio resources in the most efficient way, which means users with the best channel conditions can transmit higher data rates. The priority factor calculation for the MaxT scheduler is as follows:

$$P_k^{MaxT}(t) = argmax_k\,[SINR_k\,[t]] \qquad (6.3)$$

where $P_k^{MaxT}(t)$ is the time domain priority factor using the MaxT scheduler, k is the bearer number and $SINR_k\,[t]$ is the instantaneous SINR value of bearer k.

MaxT maximizes the cell throughput and the system performance. However, it fails to provide any fairness among the users. It often has the problem of users starvation because users that experience bad channel conditions will rarely get the chance to transmit as other users receive preference for scheduling. The MaxT also fails in guaranteeing the QoS requirements for the same reason mentioned above.

6.3 Downlink MAC Scheduler Design

The LTE MAC scheduler has a very challenging job of managing the balance between several requirements and targets. On the one hand, the radio scheduler has to differentiate and guarantee the QoS requirements (e.g., delay budget or loss ratio) of the different LTE bearer types corresponding to different services and traffic classes. On the other hand, it can aim to provide fairness among all users as well as maximize the cell throughput [ZWGTG11b].

It was discussed earlier within this chapter that the radio scheduler is divided into two stages: a Time Domain Scheduler (TDS), and a Frequency Domain Scheduler (FDS). Each of these schedulers has different target criteria. The TDS normally deals with issues related to the QoS requirements and user/bearer prioritization; whereas the FDS deals with issues related to spectrum allocation and multi-user diversity exploitation. The TDS creates a prioritized candidate list of the active users/bearers ready to transmit within the TTI, and then passes this candidate list to the FDS. Then the FDS picks up the users from the list, starting from the highest priority ones, and allocates them with the frequency resources (i.e., PRBs) in a way that exploits the different channel conditions of the different users.

The scheduler algorithm designed within this work is called Optimized Service Aware scheduler (OSA). The general OSA scheduler framework is shown in Figure 6.2. The OSA scheduler is divided into three main stages: QCI classification, TDS and FDS. Over the next subsections each of these stages will be explained in more detail.

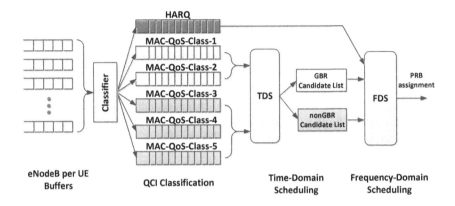

Figure 6.2: OSA general scheduler framework

6.3.1 QCI Classification

In chapter 3.5 it is shown that the 3GPP defines nine different QCIs, with four of them being defined as Guaranteed Bit Rate (GBR) bearers and five as non-Guaranteed Bit Rate (non-GBR) ones. Within the OSA scheduler framework, five different MAC-QoS-Classes are defined to differentiate and prioritize between the bearers according to their QoS class. Two classes are defined as GBR, and three as non-GBR. In addition, a high priority queue is also defined in the framework to handle pending HARQ retransmissions. The reason why five classes are defined within the OSA framework is to be able to differentiate between the five important services within the LTE network: VoIP, video conferencing, buffered video streaming, HTTP and FTP. Nevertheless, the OSA framework is open to define any number of MAC QoS classes if the operator has more services to differentiate.

Each IP bearer flow is identified with a Differentiated Services Code Point (DSCP) value, which is characterized by the Quality of Service Class Identifier (QCI) at the application level. Based on the DSCP value the scheduler maps the incoming IP packets into different MAC QoS classes. A mapping example is shown in Table 6.1.

Bearer type	Traffic example	QCI	DSCP	MAC-QoS-Class
GBR	VoIP	QCI-1	AF43 - EF	MAC-QoS-Class-1
GBR	Video Conferencing	QCI-2/4	AF42 - AF33	MAC-QoS-Class-2
non-GBR	Video Streaming	QCI-7	AF32 - AF23	MAC-QoS-Class-3
non-GBR	HTTP	QCI-8	AF22 - AF13	MAC-QoS-Class-4
non-GBR	FTP	QCI-9	AF12 and below	MAC-QoS-Class-5

Table 6.1: DSCP/QCI to MAC-QoS-Class mapping example

In each TTI, the QCI classifier identifies the active bearers, i.e., the ones that have data to transmit and then maps them to the corresponding MAC-QoS-Class. This means at the end of this process, the scheduler will have populated classes with active bearers that will be considered for this TTI transmission. One thing to notice here is the HARQ handling. Each bearer is checked first against having a pending HARQ retransmission, if that is the case, the QCI classifier will allow these bearers to perform their retransmission taking into account the amount of PRBs required for their transmission. These bearers are no longer considered for a new transmission within this TTI cycle. The retransmissions use the same amount of PRBs as the previous unsuccessful transmission as specified by the 3GPP standardization.

6.3.2 Time Domain Scheduler (TDS)

The time domain scheduler is responsible for prioritizing the bearers based on their QoS requirements. This unit is the first stage of a two-stage scheduling process. Within the first phase, no actual resources are scheduled to the users, the TDS checks the active bearers of the different MAC-QoS-Classes (that are already populated by the QCI classifier) and prioritizes them based on their urgency and requirements.

The TDS separates the bearers' prioritization process into two categories: GBR and non-GBR bearers' prioritization. In each TTI, the TDS creates two separate bearer candidate lists that are passed later to the FDS, so as to start the spectrum allocation process for that respective TTI. The candidate lists, as the name indicates, are merely suggestions for the FDS. It expresses which bearer has a higher priority to be served. The prioritization criterion within each list is different depending on the bearer type.

GBR bearer prioritization: the GBR bearers have a guaranteed rate that has to
be satisfied, and normally the GBR bearers are used for real time applications sensitive to delays. This means that these bearers should be served without any extra
delays otherwise they will lose their real time characteristics. VoIP is a typical example of such a GBR service, in which an application end-to-end delay of higher
than 150ms is already noticeable in terms of bad call quality. The OSA scheduler
prioritizes the GBR bearers based on their buffering delays at the eNodB and their
QoS class weight as follows [ZZW⁺11]:

$$P_k^{GBR}(t) = argmax_k \left[W_{QoS\_j} \times HOL_{delay\_k} \right] \qquad (6.4)$$

Here, $P_k^{GBR}(t)$ is the time domain GBR priority metric, k is the bearer number,
W_{QoS_j} is the QoS weight of the jth MAC QoS class, which is used to enforce
priorities and differentiate between QoS classes, and HOL_{delay_k} is bearer k's head-
of-line packet delay in the PDCP buffer (i.e., PDCP buffering delay).

The priority metric aims at differentiating the GBR bearers based on their QoS
class, as well as their delay. For example, a bearer of MAC-QoS-Class-1 can
be given higher priority over MAC-QoS-Class-2. Based on $P_k^{GBR}(t)$, the GBR
candidate list is generated by sorting the bearers with the highest values first. In
some cases it can be designed that the GBR bearers are not added to the GBR
candidate list, i.e., not scheduled with these TTIs, if their delays have not exceeded
a certain pre-defined threshold. Some real time services, like VoIP, can tolerate
certain delays (up to 150 ms) and thus it is not crucial to serve them immediately.
In addition, these real time services usually have small packet sizes, thus buffering
some packets together and then multiplexing them can increase the overall spectral
efficiency. Delaying the transmission of the GBR packets will increase the overall
end-to-end delay for the GBR bearers but will help in serving other non-GBR
bearers, as well as increasing the overall spectral efficiency. This will be shown
later in section 6.4.2.

non-GBR bearer prioritization: the non-GBR bearers normally carry best effort type of services such as, buffered video streaming, web browsing (i.e., HTTP),
file downloads and uploads (i.e., FTP). Such services do not have strict delay
requirements compared to the real time ones. The OSA scheduler supports up
to three different MAC-QoS-Classes to differentiate between the non-GBR services, and also provides cell throughput maximization while still maintaining fairness among the different non-GBR bearers. Again, the three defined MAC-QoS-
Classes are not a restriction and the OSA scheduler can define more MAC QoS

classes if required. The active bearers within the non-GBR MAC-QoS-Classes are prioritized by the TDS based on several criteria. The prioritization is done through calculating the non-GBR priority factor, this factor follows a similar trend like the weighted proportional fair scheduling but with some minor modifications. The main difference is the idea of exploiting the average channel conditions of the user within the priority factor calculation as follows [ZZW$^+$11]:

$$P_k^{nonGBR}(t) = argmax_k \left[W_{QoS\_j} \times \frac{\overline{\gamma_k[t]}}{\overline{\theta_k[t]}} \right] \tag{6.5}$$

where $P_k^{nonGBR}(t)$ is the time domain priority factor of the non-GBR bearers, k is the bearer number, W_{QoS_j} is the QoS weight of the jth QoS class, $\overline{\gamma_k[t]}$ is the normalized average channel condition (i.e., SINR) of bearer k and $\overline{\theta_k[t]}$ is the normalized average throughput of bearer k.

The normalized average channel condition $\overline{\gamma_k[t]}$ is a unit less measure that is normalized in the range between 0 and 1, it is calculated using the exponential moving average formula as follows:

$$\overline{\gamma_k[t]} = (1 - 1/\tau) \times \overline{\gamma_k[t-1]} + 1/\tau \times \frac{SINR_k[t]}{SINR_{max}} \tag{6.6}$$

τ is the smoothing factor of the exponential moving average window, it is set to be 1000 TTIs (i.e., 1 second), this means that the averaging function averages the SINR values from 1 second moving window from the past. $SINR_k$ is the instantaneous channel condition of the kth bearer and $SINR_{max}$ is a scaling factor used to normalize the channel condition, in order to have a unit less measure between 0 and 1.

The average throughput estimate $\overline{\theta_k[t]}$ is calculated also using the exponential moving average formula as in equation (6.2).

The QoS weight factor W_{QoS_j} is used to ensure the priority differentiation between the different non-GBR services. Table 6.2 shows the weight factor values used in this thesis.

Traffic type	MAC-QoS-Class	W_{QoS}
Video streaming	MAC-QoS-Class-3	5
HTTP	MAC-QoS-Class-4	2
FTP	MAC-QoS-Class-5	1

Table 6.2: An example of QoS weight values for different non-GBR services

The reason why these values are chosen was to differentiate between the three nonGBR services by giving HTTP twice higher priority than FTP, since the HTTP has normally smaller size compared to FTP. As for the video service a weight of 5 has been chosen in order to put it on a much higher priority than HTTP and FTP. However, LTE network operators are open to chose any QoS weight values that map their internal services differentiation policy.

6.3.3 Frequency Domain Scheduler (FDS)

The FDS is responsible for distributing the radio interface resources (PRBs) among the different bearers. Figure 6.3 shows the basic FDS flow chart. The FDS uses the candidate lists provided by the TDS to choose which bearers should be served within the specific TTIs. The candidate lists contain prioritized bearers based on their QoS requirements. The FDS starts first with the GBR candidate list, i.e., the GBR bearers are served first with strict priority over the non-GBR bearers. The FDS uses an algorithm similar to the well known round robin for the allocation process: one PRB at a time, with some channel conditions optimization. One PRB is allocated first to the highest priority GBR bearer and then another PRB is allocated to the 2nd highest bearer and so on until all PRBs are distributed. The distribution is done by assigning the bearers their best PRBs out of the spectrum; the best PRB is measured in terms of their SINR value (the higher the better). This is continued in iterations until all GBR bearers have been served within this TTI. For a certain GBR bearer to be scheduled one of two conditions must be satisfied:

1. When a new PRB is assigned for a bearer, the newly achieved data rate is checked against this bearer PDCP buffer whether or not it can empty the buffer, or in other words if the new Transport Block Size (TBS) is higher than that bearer PDCP buffer.

2. If the new iteration PRB leads to a lower TBS than the previous iteration TBS, this is possible in the case that the newly assigned PRB has a very bad SINR value that reduces the overall combined SINR into a lower value, and thus achieves a lower TBS/rate.

The first condition, evaluates whether the assigned PRBs are sufficient to empty the bearer's buffer. If that is the case there is no need of assigning any further new PRBs for that specific bearer. The second condition, checks if the newly given PRB will cause a reduction of the new TBS due to the selection of a lower MCS. Since the bearer always gets the best PRB, there is no use of keeping this bearer anymore

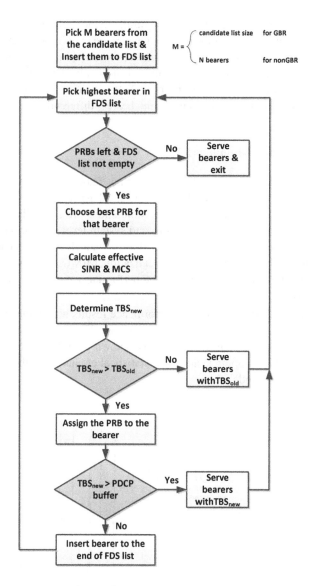

Figure 6.3: FDS general flow chart

in the scheduling iterations as all left PRBs do not have good SINR values for that bearer. Once all GBR bearers have been scheduled the non-GBR scheduling starts.

Scheduling the non-GBR bearers is very similar to the GBR procedure with only one difference: only a subset of non-GBR bearers are chosen out of the non-GBR candidate list for the PRBs iterative allocation procedure, instead of the complete candidate list, as in the GBR case. This subset is normally chosen to be the highest number of non-GBR bearers ψ in the non-GBR candidate list. ψ is an integer value and is related to the fairness among the bearers differentiation.

6.3.4 Link-to-System Mapping (L2S)

In wireless network simulation, it is normally not feasible to simulate in details both physical layer aspects, as well as network level aspects at the same time due to the huge complexity involved. Hence, simulations are normally divided into two different levels: link level simulations and system level simulations. The link level simulations focus on the wireless medium (channel) and physical layer aspects, like modulation, channel coding, equalization, MIMO, etc. The system level simulations, on the other hand, focus on the performance evaluations of the upper layer protocols and network performance.

In order to have accurate network performance results within the system level simulations, some link level emulation is required. This is normally done using mapping techniques between the two levels, known as link-to-system mapping. With the help of this mapping technique a statistical emulation of the Block Error Rate (BLER) can be modeled.

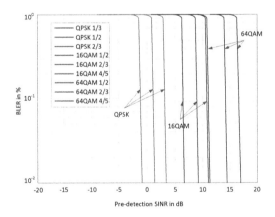

Figure 6.4: Reference BLER versus SINR AWGN curves

Within the literature, two methods are mainly used to achieve the mapping: Average Value Interface and the Actual Value Interface (AVI) [HSH$^+$97]. The AVI method is used to map the SINR value emulated by the system level simulation on the Additive White Gaussian Noise (AWGN) curves to check what modulation and coding scheme can be used to obtain a transmission with a certain target BLER. Figure 6.4 shows reference AWGN BLER versus SINR curves for different MCS. For example, when the instantaneous SINR value is 5 dB, then using MCS of QPSK 2/3, can achieve a transmission with a BLER lower than 10%, whereas using MCS of 16QAM 1/2 it will not be possible to achieve a transmission with the target 10% BLER. If there is only one target BLER within the simulation then having only a reference table will be enough, where for each MCS a target SINR value is given.

In LTE, the legacy AVI method cannot be applied directly and some modifications are required to make it applicable. As highlighted before, LTE uses OFDMA as the transmission scheme for the downlink, and this means that a UE can get several frequency resources (i.e., PRBs) for a single transmission. Each of these PRBs might have a different SINR value, depending on the channel conditions that each experiences, and all of these SINR values must be combined together to form a single SINR value that can be mapped to the AWGN curves. Several methods in literature are used to combine the multi-carrier SINR values, and two of the most widely used ones that have been proven to be accurate are: Exponential Effective SINR Mapping (EESM) and Mutual Information Effective SINR Mapping (MIESM). The difference between the two methods can be found in [BAS$^+$05]. For this thesis work, the EESM method is chosen due to its simpler implementation and less complex computational cost.

For the mapping of the several SINR values into a single effective SINR value to work properly, it is very important that the following approximation is valid for every instantaneous channel realization and not "on average" for a given channel model [Zah11]:

$$BLEP\left(\{\gamma_k\}\right) \approx BLEP_{AWGN}\left(\gamma_{eff}\right) \qquad (6.7)$$

where $BLEP\left(\{\gamma_k\}\right)$ is the instantaneous BLock Error Probability for the channel state $\{\gamma_k\}$ and $BLEP_{AWGN}\left(\gamma_{eff}\right)$ is the AWGN BLock Error Probability.

That is why a scaling factor β is defined for each MCS in order to fulfill equation (6.7). The Effective SINR mapping is calculated as follows:

$$SINR_{eff} = I^{-1} \left(\frac{1}{N} \sum_{n=1}^{N} I\left(SINR_n\right) \right) \tag{6.8}$$

where, $I(x)$ is known as the information measure function and $I^{-1}(x)$ is its inverse. The EESM defines the information function $I(x)$ and $I^{-1}(x)$ as follows:

$$\begin{aligned} I(x) &= exp\left(-\frac{x}{\beta}\right) \\ I^{-1}(x) &= -\beta ln(x) \end{aligned} \tag{6.9}$$

Now, substituting equation 6.9 in 6.8 the effective SINR calculation according to the EESM method is:

$$SINR_{eff} = -\beta ln \left[\frac{1}{N} \sum_{n=1}^{N} exp\left(-\frac{SINR_n}{\beta} \right) \right] \tag{6.10}$$

where N is the total number of PRBs given to a UE, $SINR_n$ is the SINR value of the nth PRB and β is the MCS dependent scaling factor. The different β values can be found in Table 6.3.

MCS	QPSK	QPSK	QPSK	QPSK	QPSK
β	1.4	1.44	1.48	1.5	1.62
MCS	16QAM	16QAM	16QAM	16QAM	16QAM
β	3.10	4.32	5.37	7.71	15.5
MCS	64QAM	64QAM	64QAM	64QAM	
β	19.6	24.7	27.6	28	

Table 6.3: β values for each MCS [KSW$^+$08][LV08a][Val06]

Once the effective SINR value has been calculated and checked against the AWGN curves, the appropriate MCS is determined for this set of PRBs. Using the number of PRBs and the MCS, the corresponding transport block size can be found from the standardized 3GPP table [36.10a] (see Table A.1).

6.3.5 HARQ Modeling

The HARQ functionality is modeled by linking it to some extent to the MAC scheduler. Every bearer has 8 stop-and-wait HARQ processes [36.10a]. This means that when a packet is unsuccessfully transmitted over the air interface it has to wait at least 8ms to be retransmitted.

The HARQ modeling is done through a statistical method, where for every transmission a uniformly distributed random number between 0 and 1 is generated. This number represents the probability of the packet being transmitted successfully. This number is compared against the target BLER to determine the transmission probability of the packet. Three different HARQ BLERs are defined: One for the 1st transmission, one for the 1st retransmission and one for the 2nd retransmission as shown in Table 6.4.

It can be seen that the BLER numbers decrease with the retransmissions, until it reaches 0% (successful transmission) for the 2nd retransmission. The reason for this simplified modeling is the fact that in LTE chase combining with incremental redundancy is used to decode the received packets, this means that each new retransmission is combined with the older unsuccessful transmission and the probability of decoding successfully increases.

	1st **transmission**	1st **retransmission**	2nd **retransmission**
BLER	10%	1%	0%

Table 6.4: BLER and HARQ transmissions

6.4 Downlink MAC Scheduler Analysis

The purpose of this section is to study and analyze performance of the Optimized Service Aware scheduler (OSA), which is proposed by this thesis. In order to investigate the benefits of the OSA scheduler and to see where it lies in the trade-off metric. First, a comparison between the OSA and the most classical schedulers (BET and MaxT) is studied. Next, some of the key aspects of the OSA are presented with a detailed analysis of the scheduler performance in terms of fairness, QoS guarantees and the exploitation of the different channel conditions (i.e., multi-user diversity). In the last analysis, the benefits of the real time GBR delay sensitivity exploitation is discussed, highlighting the additional gains that can be achieved by delaying the GBR services to some extent without harming their QoS or their performance.

6.4.1 OSA vs. Classical Schedulers

In this section, the OSA scheduler is compared against two of the classical schedulers: Blind Equal Throughput (BET) and Maximum Throughput (MaxT). The reason why these two schedulers are chosen for the comparison is that each represents the upper limit of some scheduling characteristics. The BET focuses on fairness and tries to allocate resources in such a way that the overall throughput of each user is the same. But the MaxT focuses on maximizing the cell throughput and allocates as many resources as possible to users in best channel conditions as long as they have data to transmit. By doing so, the spectral efficiency can be significantly enhanced. However, the fairness between the scheduled users is completely lost.

6.4.1.1 FTP Only Scenario

The scenario is configured with a varying number of FTP users, ranging from 5 to 40 FTP users. Each scenario is repeated with the same parameters for each of the three schedulers (OSA, BET and MaxT). The detailed simulation configuration can be seen in Table 6.5.

Parameter	Configurations
Total Number of PRBs (Spectrum)	25 PRBs (5 MHz)
Mobility model	Random Way Point (RWP) with 120 km/h
Number of users	5, 10, 15, 20, 25, 30 and 40 FTP users
Channel model	described in section 4.3.5
MAC Scheduler	TDS: OSA, BET and MaxT FDS: Iterative RR approach 6.3.3 max number of nonGBR UEs served per TTI: 5
HARQ	Modeled as in Table 6.4
FTP traffic model	FTP File size: constant 20 MByte As soon as one file finishes the next FTP file is started immediately.
Simulation run time	2000 seconds

Table 6.5: Simulation configurations

The average user FTP download time is shown in Figure 6.5. It can be seen that all three schedulers start with the same average user FTP download time in the 5 users scenario, since the FDS is configured with 5 nonGBR users to be served per TTI. Both the OSA and BET schedulers show very good fairness between the users. This can be seen by the small standard deviation error bars which means that all the users achieve similar download time.

The OSA scheduler performs better than the BET, as expected, as it also takes into account the user channel conditions when scheduling. The MaxT scheduler shows the smallest average FTP download time compared to the OSA and BET, as it always schedules the users in the best channel conditions resulting in much better spectral efficiency and thus higher throughput. The MaxT scheduler has much higher standard deviation (higher unfairness), this is the expected behavior of the MaxT scheduler since it only schedules users with the best instantaneous channel conditions, so some users are preferred than others which will lead to a higher unfairness between them.

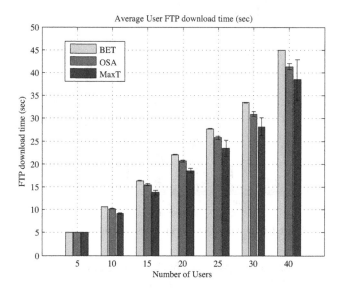

Figure 6.5: Average user FTP download time

Figure 6.6 shows the unfairness factor in the user's average FTP download time. An unfairness factor UF% is defined to represent in percentage the level of unfairness between the user download times, it is calculated as follows [Wee11]:

$$UF\% = \frac{\frac{1}{N} \cdot \sum_{i=1}^{N} \left| T_i - T_{avg} \right|}{T_{avg}} \times 100 \qquad (6.11)$$

where T_i is the individual per-user average download time and T_{avg} is the average of all user download times. A higher unfairness factor implies a higher level of unfairness.

The figures show that both OSA and BET have very good fairness between the users that is almost less than 1.5% in all cases. The MaxT scheduler suffers from much higher unfairness among the users. The unfairness increases with the increasing number of users because only users with best channel conditions are scheduled and the ones with bad channel conditions are rarely served.

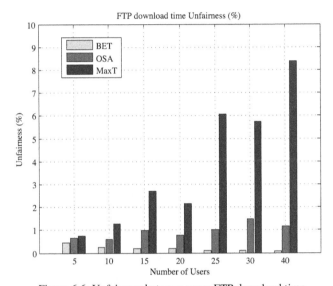

Figure 6.6: Unfairness between users FTP download time

The system performance represented by the achieved average cell throughput is shown in Figure 6.7. It can be seen that the MaxT scheduler achieves the highest average cell throughput. Of course, this is due to the fact that the MaxT scheduler has a much better spectral efficiency since it schedules users with the best instantaneous channel conditions, and thus the scheduled users transmit with higher MCS because of their good channel conditions. The cell throughput increases with increasing the total number of FTP users in the system, because the probability of finding 5 FTP users with best channel condition in each TTI is much higher when there are more users in the system.

The BET has the worst cell throughput, moreover, the cell throughput tends to decrease with a much faster pace when increasing the number of users. This is because for BET is exactly the opposite (compared to MaxT), the probability of having users with bad channel conditions also increases with increasing the number of users. Since the BET scheduler tries to equalize the achieved throughput to be the same for all users, it has to give more resources to users with bad channel conditions as their transmission is performed with much lower MCS and thus lower spectral efficiency.

The OSA scheduler represents the proper balance between fairness and spectral efficiency. It can be seen that the cell throughput achieved is lower than the MaxT, but higher than the BET. The cell throughput slightly decreases when the number of users is increased from 5 to 15 and then it stabilizes.

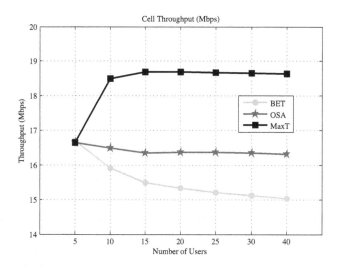

Figure 6.7: Average cell throughput comparison

Figure 6.8 shows the spider web graph of the result comparison for the scenario with 40 users. Within this graph, there are three different axes: FTP application throughput, fairness percentage and cell throughput. The fairness shown in this figure is simply the inverse of the unfairness factor described in equation 6.11 (i.e., 100% - UF%). The FTP application throughput is calculated by dividing the FTP file size by the FTP file download time. The BET shows the worst performance, although it has the highest fairness among the schedulers it fails to achieve high throughputs due to the bad spectral efficiency. The OSA scheduler performs better than the BET, as it has higher application and cell throughput with slightly reduced fairness. Although the MaxT has the highest cell throughput it fails to provide the necessary fairness balance between the users and suffers from high unfairness.

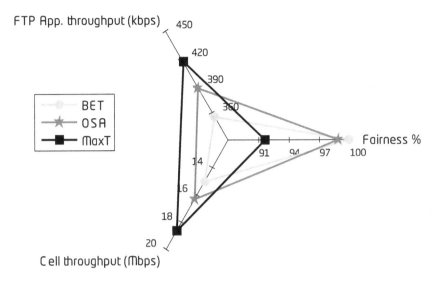

Figure 6.8: 40 UE scenario - scheduler comparison

The results shown in the figure above can be interpreted in the following manner, the larger the shape of each scheduler is (in this case the graph is the triangular shape) the better that scheduler performs. This is because the higher the value recorded on each axis is the better is the performance. For example, the cell throughput axis shows the achieved cell throughput for each of the three schedulers and the MaxT has the highest cell throughput, whereas the BET has the lowest one. The results show that OSA achieves the best relative performance. Although it has a relatively lower FTP and cell throughput compared to the MaxT, it succeeds in providing the necessary fairness between the scheduled users.

6.4.1.2 Mixed Traffic Scenario

This scenario is configured with users of mixed traffic types: VoIP, Video, HTTP and FTP. The performance of the three schedulers (OSA, w-BET and w-MaxT) are compared against each other using the mixed traffic scenario. The weighted BET/MaxT are modified versions of the classical schedulers (see section 6.2.1) so that a fair comparison to the OSA scheduler is possible. The priority metrics of these two modified schedulers are defined as follows:

$$P_k^{w-BET}(t) = argmax_k \left[\frac{W_{QoS\_j}}{\overline{\theta_k[t]}} \right]$$
$$P_k^{w-MaxT}(t) = argmax_k \left[W_{QoS\_j} \times [SINR_k[t]] \right] \tag{6.12}$$

where $P_k(t)$ is the time domain priority factor, k is the bearer number, $\overline{\theta_k[t]}$ is the normalized average throughput of bearer k, which is calculated in the same way as in equation (6.2), $SINR_k[t]$ is the instantaneous SINR value of bearer k and W_{QoS_j} is the weight factor of the jth QoS class.

The simulation configurations can be seen in Table 6.6. As can be noticed from the name, the two classical schedulers are slightly modified by adding the QoS weight to provide the QoS differentiation in order to have a fair comparison.

Parameter	Configurations
Total Number of PRBs (Spectrum)	25 PRBs (5 MHz)
Mobility model	Random Way Point (RWP) with vehicular speed
Number of users	40 VoIP, 20 Video, 20 HTTP and 20 FTP users
Channel model	described in section 4.3.5
MAC Scheduler	TDS: OSA, w-BET and w-MaxT
	QoS weights as defined in Table 6.2
	FDS: Iterative RR approach 6.3.3
	max number of nonGBR UEs served per TTI: 5
Traffic QoS mapping	VoIP is mapped to MAC-QoS-Class 1
	Video is mapped to MAC-QoS-Class 3
	HTTP is mapped to MAC-QoS-Class 4
	FTP is mapped to MAC-QoS-Class 5
HARQ	Modeled as in Table 6.4
VoIP traffic model	Silence/Talk Spurt length = negative exponential distribution with 3 seconds mean
	Encoder Scheme: GSM EFR with rate 12.2 kbps
	Continuous call throughout the whole simulation time
Video traffic model	24 Frames per second with frame size: 1333 bytes
	Data rate: 256 kbps
HTTP traffic model	Number of pages per session: 1 page
	Number of objects in a page: 1 object
	Object size: constant 100 KBytes
	Reading time: constant 12 seconds
FTP traffic model	FTP File size: constant 5 MByte
	As soon as one file finishes the next FTP file is started.
Simulation run time	2000 seconds

Table 6.6: Simulation configurations

Figure 6.9 shows the spider web graph for the comparison of the different application delays for each of the different schedulers. The graph has four different axes, each representing a specific application delay performance: VoIP application end-to-end delay, Video application end-to-end delay, HTTP page response time and FTP file download time. Since all of the axes represent delays, then the smaller the spider web shape the better the performance is.

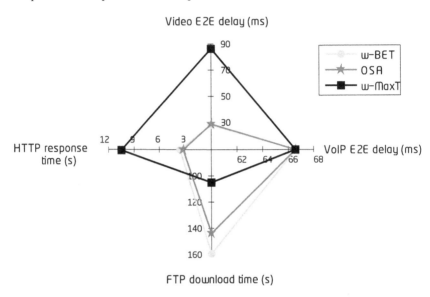

Figure 6.9: Application delay performance comparison between schedulers

The VoIP end-to-end delay is the same for all the three different schedulers, because the VoIP is mapped to the highest GBR MAC-QoS-Class. This means, VoIP users are served with strict priority before serving any other users for all schedulers. Although the w-MaxT scheduler shows the best FTP file download time, it has the highest end-to-end delay for the video application, as well as the highest HTTP page response time. The w-MaxT scheduler fails in providing the necessary QoS differentiation, even though a QoS dependent weight is added to the original MaxT criteria. It still focuses on serving the users with the best instantaneous channel conditions, leading to a better FTP performance. Both OSA and w-BET, provide good results for the video and HTTP users, however, the OSA scheduler outperforms the w-BET scheduler when looking at the FTP download time due to the better spectral efficiency and being more aware of the user channel diversity.

In summary, the spider web graph shows that the OSA scheduler provides the right
balance between performance and QoS differentiation.

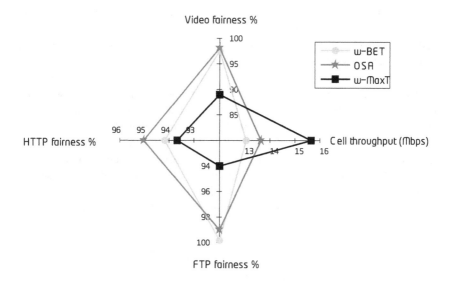

Figure 6.10: Fairness and cell throughput comparison between schedulers

Figure 6.10 compares the schedulers in terms of fairness and cell throughput.
The fairness is measured in terms of how similar the user performance of each
class is, i.e., if the fairness is 100%, it means that all the users achieve the same
end-to-end results. It is calculated as 100% - UF% (for UF% see equation (6.11).
As expected, the w-MaxT shows the worst fairness between the users in all three
different nonGBR traffic classes (i.e., video, HTTP and FTP). The OSA scheduler
provides very good fairness among the users for each traffic class. Looking at the
cell throughput, it can be seen that the w-MaxT achieves the highest cell throughput since it focuses only on exploiting the best instantaneous channel conditions,
leading to a better spectral efficiency and thus a better cell throughput. The OSA
has lower cell throughput than the w-MaxT, but still higher than the w-BET. This
is to be expected, as it is always a trade-off between cell throughput and the user
fairness. In this case, a relatively lower cell throughput is the penalty that the OSA
scheduler has to pay, to achieve better QoS differentiation between the services.

6.4.2 GBR Delay Exploitation

This analysis studies what happens if the GBR services are intentionally delayed up to their QoS requirements. The aim of the study is to see if any benefit can be gained while still having acceptable GBR service performance. The intended GBR service to be delayed is the VoIP service. The reason why the VoIP service is chosen is because it is normally served with strict priority, which might lead to worse spectral efficiency due to the small VoIP data volume that is sent over the air interface. In other words, delaying the VoIP packets for some time will lead to a better spectral efficiency (higher cell throughput) due to packet multiplexing. The scenarios are configured based on the additional delay of the VoIP packets. The LTE MAC scheduler checks in each TTI the PDCP buffer head-of-line packet delay for every VoIP user (i.e., the buffering delay of the first packet in the buffer). If the delay exceeds the pre-defined buffering delay then this VoIP user is served within this TTI. If the VoIP user is chosen to be served, the scheduler will try to allocate enough resources to finish this user's buffer. The simulation parameters for this analysis is shown in Table 6.7.

Parameter	Assumption
Total Number of PRBs (Spectrum)	25 PRBs (5 MHz)
Mobility model	Random Way Point (RWP) with vehicular speed
Number of users	40 VoIP, 20 Video, 20 HTTP and 20 FTP users
Channel model	described in section 4.3.5
MAC Scheduler	TDS: OSA; FDS: Iterative RR approach 6.3.3 # nonGBR users served per TTI: 5 users
Traffic QoS mapping HARQ and Traffic models	Similar to Table 6.6
Scenarios	sc1 (0ms): the VoIP service is served strictly without any delays sc2 (20ms): the VoIP service is delayed up to 20ms sc3 (50ms): the VoIP service is delayed up to 50ms sc4 (75ms): the VoIP service is delayed up to 75ms sc5 (100ms): the VoIP service is delayed up to 100ms sc6 (150ms): the VoIP service is delayed up to 150ms sc7 (200ms): the VoIP service is delayed up to 200ms
Simulation run time	2000 seconds

Table 6.7: Simulation configurations

Figure 6.11 shows the system cell throughput of all scenarios. It can be seen that by increasing the buffering delay of the VoIP service the cell throughput increases.

The reason for this increase is the better spectral efficiency, as multiple VoIP packets are multiplexed together in the transmission due to the additional buffering delay introduced by the scheduler. In addition, the FTP users are assigned slightly more resources for their transmission as the VoIP users are not scheduled every TTI, and thus the FTP users can transmit more bits using the additionally saved PRBs, leading to higher spectral efficiency and higher cell throughput.

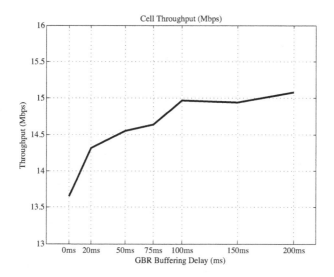

Figure 6.11: Average cell throughput

The VoIP user performance in terms of packet end-to-end delay is shown in Figure 6.12. As expected, the results show that with increasing the buffering delay of the VoIP packets, the application end-to-end delay increase. In order to evaluate the performance of the VoIP traffic, the average MOS value for each scenario is shown in Figure 6.13. The results show that the VoIP performance is slightly reduced by increasing the VoIP buffering delay, almost up to a delay threshold of about 100ms, where the call is still of acceptable quality. After the 100 ms the quality of the voice call is degraded, and is not acceptable anymore. This gives a margin that the scheduler design can exploit by delaying the VoIP services, as they can tolerate a certain delay threshold. Thus, the scheduler will be able to schedule other non-GBR bearers and increase the overall spectral efficiency.

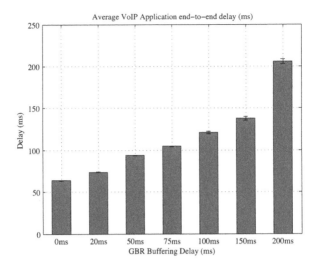

Figure 6.12: Average VoIP application end-to-end delay

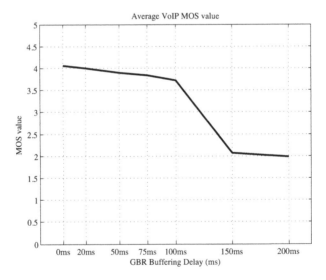

Figure 6.13: Average VoIP MOS value

The performance of the other three QoS classes (Video, HTTP and FTP) are shown in Figure 6.14. In this figure only five of the scenarios are shown, excluding the 150ms and 200ms scenario. These two scenarios are excluded as they showed unacceptable performance results for the VoIP services. The spiderweb chart shows the performance of the Video, HTTP and FTP in terms of end-to-end delay, response time, and download time respectively. Of course, the lower these values are the better the performance is, or in other words, the smaller the spiderweb shape is, the better the performance. As expected, the results show that by increasing the VoIP buffering delay, the non-GBR service performance is enhanced.

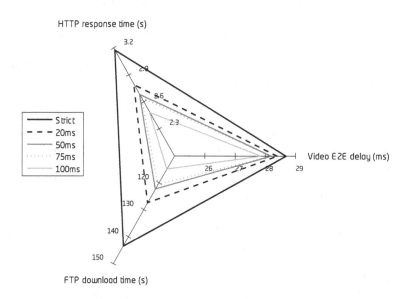

Figure 6.14: non-GBR services performance comparison spider chart

In summary, the scheduler is able to exploit some of the GBR service (VoIP in this case) characteristics and their tolerance to certain delay margins, by delaying their scheduling and additionally buffering their packets. By doing so the scheduler is able to enhance the overall system throughput due to the enhanced spectral efficiency. In addition, the non-GBR service performance is also enhanced.

6.5 Conclusion

This chapter focused on the design and implementation of an Optimized Service Aware (OSA) LTE downlink radio scheduler. The OSA scheduler is designed with de-coupled Time and Frequency Domain schedulers (TDS and FDS), the main design target behind the scheduler is to provide QoS differentiations to the different LTE services while at the same time ensuring relative fairness and optimum spectral efficiency.

The OSA scheduler is investigated in several simulation analyses, in order to study its behavior in different situations, and to highlight its performance gains. At first the OSA scheduler is compared against other classical schedulers, e.g. Maximum Throughput (MaxT), and Blind Equal Throughput (BET), with two kind of traffic scenarios: one without service differentiations by having FTP only users, and one with a traffic mix of several services (VoIP, video, HTTP and FTP). The results showed that the OSA scheduler outperforms the other two schedulers in providing the correct balance between fairness and spectral efficiency, which is something that both other schedulers fail to provide.

Another investigation, that was analyzed in this chapter, showed the potential gain that can be achieved by delaying the scheduling of the GBR services (mainly VoIP services) up to a certain threshold. The simulation scenarios were configured with different VoIP delay thresholds. The idea behind these scenarios was to study the effects of the buffering delay on the VoIP service and see to what extent does the VoIP service can tolerate these delays without any degradation on their QoS. In addition, the benefits that can arise from delaying the VoIP services were also studied. The results showed that all other nonGBR bearers have gained from delaying the VoIP bearers, where the average delays values were reduced with increasing the delay of the VoIP packets. This is due to the fact that when the VoIP services are delayed, their additional resources (i.e., PRBs) are free to be used by the other services. In addition, a significant gain in the overall cell throughput was achieved due to the better resource utilizations and the better spectral efficiency.

7 Analytical Modeling of the LTE Radio Scheduler

The main motivation behind developing an analytical model is to evaluate the system performance. Normally, the modeled system is of complex nature, and is evaluated using either simulations or real life experiments that are too exhaustive and consumes large computation power and time. In addition, real life experiments are not always possible to perform. That is why, the target behind modeling a system analytically is to approximate the system behavior mathematically and to do performance evaluations with much smaller processing effort and time.

In this chapter, several analytical LTE radio scheduler models are proposed. The models represent different LTE time domain schedulers, mainly: MaxT, BET and OSA. In addition to the Time Domain Scheduler (TDS) type, two different model categories are presented: a single class model and a two classes model. In the single class model as the name suggests, only a single traffic class is considered with no QoS differentiation. Whereas, the two classes model supports QoS differentiation between the two classes.

The analytical models developed in this thesis are based on the general WiMax analytical model proposed by [DBMC10]. However, several extensions and modifications have been applied to the [DBMC10] model by this thesis work in order to: reflect the LTE context, be able to model different LTE TDS schedulers and most importantly provide QoS differentiations between the traffic classes. This chapter is organized as follows. In section 7.1, the general analytical model as well as the performance analysis of the model are explained. Then in section 7.2 the LTE downlink scheduler analytical models are introduced, in which the single class model is described and analyzed firstly in section 7.2.1 followed by the two-dimensional model in section 7.2.3. Finally, section 7.3 concludes the chapter with the outlook highlighted at the end.

7.1 General Analytical Model

The LTE radio scheduler distributes the frequency resources, i.e., PRBs among the active users in every TTI (1 ms). There are a number of input parameters that are used by the scheduler to base the distribution decision upon, e.g., channel conditions, accumulated data rates and QoS. The scheduler uses these input parameters differently based on the scheduler type. Most schedulers consider user channel conditions as one of the main input parameters in the decision process. The channel conditions change based on the user mobility and location. The channel conditions change stochastically and the scheduler does not have control over them.

In LTE, a user can transmit data using different modulation and coding schemes (MSC). The choice of the transmission scheme depends on the channel condition or the received power, i.e. SINR value. The 3GPP standards define several MCSs that a user can transmit with. Assuming that an operator chooses to support K different MCSs, then each user can be in any of these MCSs at a given time interval of the system. In other words, a user can use MCS_k, $0 \leq k \leq K$, where MCS_0 is the outage MCS (user cannot transmit anything) and MCS_K is the maximum MCS defined by the system.

In order to model the LTE radio scheduler analytically, a multidimensional Continuous Time Markov Chain (CTMC) with state vector $(n_0, ..., n_K)$ is the most straight forward solution [DBMC10]. The state describes for each MCS, the number of users n_k that can support a certain MCS_k. The derivation of the model transitions is easy, however, the number of states (model resolution complexity) becomes very large for any realistic value of K.

Following [DBMC10], a work around for the complexity can be applied by aggregating the state description into a single dimension, where the Markov chain state n represents the number of active users in the system regardless of their MCS. The Continuous Time Markov Chain (CTMC) is composed of N+1 states as shown in Figure 7.1, with N being the total number of users in the system.

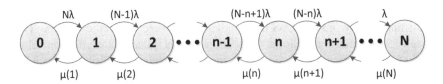

Figure 7.1: General Continuous Time Markov Chain (CTMC)

The figure shows a finite Markov chain limited by the total number of users in the system N. Each state (apart from state 0 and N) has two transitions, either going to the next state or to the previous state. Since the state itself represents the number of active users n, which is normally a subset of the total number of users N, then a transition from state n to n+1 would mean that one of the inactive users (N-n represents the number of inactive users in state n) has finished its OFF period and is now ready to transmit. On the other hand, a transition from state n to n-1 would mean that one of the active users has finished its transmission and is now switching to the inactive state.

These transitions depend on the traffic model. Within the analytical model, an infinite length ON/OFF elastic traffic model is used [DBMC10]. Such a traffic model is used to model best effort traffic, e.g., web browsing or file download. The ON part of the model represents the downloading of a file, where the duration depends on the system parameters, e.g., load, bandwidth, number of users and channel quality. The OFF period represents the reading time of the downloaded file, for example, the time the user takes to read a web page before requesting the next page. This OFF period is independent of the system parameters. The ON period is represented by the file size $(\overline{X_{on}})$, whereas the OFF period is represented by the OFF duration $(\overline{t_{off}})$, both are assumed to be exponentially distributed [DBMC10].

With the infinite ON/OFF traffic model, a transition from state n to n+1 is performed with the rate $(N - n)\lambda$, with λ being the inverse of the average reading time or the file inter-arrival time:

$$\lambda = \frac{1}{\overline{t_{off}}} \qquad (7.1)$$

The transition from state n to n-1 is performed with the generic rate $\mu(n)$ (i.e., departure rate), since the ON period depends on the system state (as explained earlier) which in this case depends on the state with n active users.

The work around provides a reduction in the number of states (model resolution complexity) to a small number that depends only on the total number of users in the system. Nevertheless, the complexity is now moved from the Markov chain states into the departure rate $\mu(n)$ which depends on the scheduling discipline.

7.1.1 Performance Evaluation

The general analytical model depends upon two input parameters: arrival transition rate λ and the generic departure transition rate $\mu(n)$ as shown in Figure 7.1.

Assuming that the generic $\mu(n)$ can be estimated, the Markov chain steady state probability $\pi(n)$ can be evaluated as follows [Kle76]:

$$\pi \cdot \mathbf{Q} = 0 \tag{7.2}$$

where π is a vector representing the steady state probability of the Markov chain, i.e., $\pi = [\pi_0, \pi_1, \ldots \pi_N]$ and $\sum_i \pi_i = 1$; $\mathbf{Q}$ is the infinitesimal generator, which is a matrix of the transition rates as follows:

$$\mathbf{Q} = \begin{bmatrix} -N\lambda & N\lambda & 0 & 0 & 0 \\ \mu(1) & -((N-1)\lambda + \mu(1)) & (N-1)\lambda & 0 & 0 \\ 0 & \mu(2) & -((N-2)\lambda + \mu(2)) & (N-2)\lambda & 0 & \ldots \\ & & \cdot & & \\ & & \cdot & & \\ & & \cdot & & \end{bmatrix}$$

It can be seen in the infinitesimal matrix $\mathbf{Q}$ that the diagonal values are set to the negative value of the sum of the row. This is because the sum of each row in $\mathbf{Q}$ should be zero [Kle76], i.e., $\sum_j q_{ij} = 0$ for all i. where the diagonal values (i.e., q_{ii}) represents the state self transition rate.

Equation 7.2 can be solved using the replace-one-equation method [Ste94]. An alternative to solving equation 7.2 is to use the closed loop solution for the steady state probability $\pi(n)$, which is derived from the birth-and-death structure of the Markov chain [DBMC10], and is as follows:

$$\pi(n) = \left(\prod_{i=1}^{n} \frac{(N-i+1)\lambda}{\mu(i)} \right) \pi(0) \tag{7.3}$$

where $\pi(0)$ is obtained by normalization.

Once the steady state probabilities have been calculated, the system performance evaluation can be evaluated. First of all, the average number of active users in the system $\overline{Q}$ is calculated. As $\overline{Q}$ is the mean number of users and $\pi(n)$ is the probability of every state, i.e. probability of having n active users, then $\overline{Q}$ will be:

$$\overline{Q} = \sum_{n=1}^{N} n\pi(n) \tag{7.4}$$

Next, the mean number of departures by unit time $\overline{D}$ is calculated as follows:

$$\overline{D} = \sum_{n=1}^{N} \mu(n)\pi(n) \tag{7.5}$$

And finally, according to Little's law [Ste11], the average ON duration, i.e. the average file download time can be expressed as:

$$\overline{t_{on}} = \frac{\overline{Q}}{\overline{D}} \tag{7.6}$$

Another possible way to calculate the average ON duration $\overline{t_{on}}$ would be to divide the mean number of users $\overline{Q}$ by the mean number of arrivals per unit time $\overline{\lambda}$, which can be expressed as:

$$\overline{\lambda} = \sum_{n=1}^{N} (N - n + 1)\lambda \cdot \pi(n) \tag{7.7}$$

Thus, the average file download time will be:

$$\overline{t_{on}} = \frac{\overline{Q}}{\overline{\lambda}} \tag{7.8}$$

7.1.2 Generic Departure Rate

$\mu(n)$ represents the average departure rate out of state n, thus it depends on the number of active users, the system bandwidth, scheduler discipline, file size and the system transmission interval. In the context of LTE, the transmission interval is 1ms. A departure from state n to n-1 happens when one of the n active users in that state finishes its file, and thus $\mu(n)$ is estimated as follows [DBMC10]:

$$\mu(n) = \frac{\overline{TBS}(n)}{\overline{X_{on}} \cdot TTI} \tag{7.9}$$

where $\overline{TBS}(n)$ is the average number of bits transmitted within a TTI, when n users are active. $\overline{TBS}(n)$ represents the average amount of bits sent for all users served within a TTI. $\overline{X_{on}}$ is the average file size of the ON period.

$\overline{TBS}(n)$ depends on several system parameters. It depends on the MCS used by the system, the number of active users n and the scheduling discipline. Within this general analytical model, each MCS has a stationary probability P_k that represents the probability of a user to be able to use a certain MCS_k. This stationary probability is estimated through simulations using a predefined scenario for a certain environment, with a certain mobility model and a certain transmission power. $\overline{TBS}(n)$ can be expressed as follows:

$$\overline{TBS}(n) = \sum_{\substack{(n_0,...,n_K)=(0,...,0)| \\ n_0+...+n_K=n \\ n_0 \neq n}}^{(n,...,n)} \overline{TBS}(n_0,...,n_K) \begin{pmatrix} n \\ n_0,...,n_K \end{pmatrix} \left[\prod_{k=0}^{K} P_k^{n_k} \right] \qquad (7.10)$$

where $\begin{pmatrix} n \\ n_0,...,n_K \end{pmatrix}$ is the multinomial coefficient, P_k is the stationary probability of MCS_k, n_k is the number of active users in MCS_k (with MCS_0 and n_0
representing the outage probability and the number of active users that are in outage), and $\overline{TBS}(n_0,...,n_K)$ is the total number of bits transmitted for all served users
under the specific combination $(n_0,...,n_K)$, it is calculated as follows:

$$\overline{TBS}(n_0,...,n_K) = \sum_{k=1}^{K} \sum_{\substack{i=1 \\ n_k \neq 0}}^{n_k} TBS_k(\eta) \cdot X_{k,i} \qquad (7.11)$$

$$X_{k,i} = \begin{cases} 1 & \text{if } UE_{k,i} \text{ is served} \\ 0 & \text{else} \end{cases} \quad \text{with} \quad \sum_k \sum_i X_{k,i} = \eta \qquad (7.12)$$

where η is the number of users served within the certain combination $(n_0,...,n_K)$,
$TBS_k(\eta)$ is the number of bits that can be transmitted by one served user (out of the
η served users) with MCS_k. TBS_k depends on η because the number of allocated
PRBs a user gets depends on the frequency domain scheduler, that distributes the
PRBs among the η users. $X_{k,i}$ represents the scheduler decision, whether the user
is served or not (1 for being served and zero otherwise).

Equation 7.10 is deducted from [DBMC10], further details on the derivation
procedure can be found in the above reference. As for equations 7.11 and 7.12,
the author of the thesis has modified the original equations in [DBMC10] so that
it can fit the modeling of the TD and FD schedulers in LTE. The main difference
between the equations is that in [DBMC10] all active users are scheduled in every
scheduling frame, whereas, the modified version serves only a subset of users in
every scheduling time frame and the choice of those users depends on the time
domain scheduler discipline.

Now, in order to understand the equations shown above, it is better to explain
each part separately. Lets first start with the summation in equation 7.10, the summation covers all possible combinations, where the n active users can be in the
modulation and coding array $(n_0,...,n_K)$, for example n=2 and K=2 then 27 different combinations are possible, however only five are valid (see Table 7.1).

possibility:	$(n_0$	n_1	$n_2)$	valid
(1)	0	0	0	
(2)	0	0	1	
(3)	0	0	2	X
(4)	0	1	0	
(5)	0	1	1	X
(6)	0	1	2	
(7)	0	2	0	X
(8)	0	2	1	
(9)	0	2	2	
(10)	1	0	0	
(11)	1	0	1	X
(12)	1	0	2	
(13)	1	1	0	X
(14)	1	1	1	
(15)	1	1	2	
(16)	1	2	0	
(17)	1	2	1	
(18)	1	2	2	
(19)	2	0	0	
(20)	2	0	1	
(21)	2	0	2	
(22)	2	1	0	
(23)	2	1	1	
(24)	2	1	2	
(25)	2	2	0	
(26)	2	2	1	
(27)	2	2	2	

Table 7.1: n=2, K=2 combinations example

This is because the summation has two additional requirements: the summations of n_k should be equal to n, i.e., all n active users should be present in the combination, and n_0 shall never hold all n active users because otherwise there will be no transmission.

$\overline{TBS}(n_0, ..., n_K)$ is the total number of bits sent for the specific combination $(n_0, ..., n_K)$, this is calculated using equation 7.11 where only a subset of the users out of the n total active users are chosen for the scheduling, the chosen η users depend on the time domain scheduling. For example, if the TD scheduler is a MaxT scheduler then the η users will be the ones with the highest MCS (i.e., highest SINR). The η number depends upon the frequency domain scheduler which is a round robin scheduler that distributes the PRBs equally among the scheduled users. It can be seen that TBS_k depends on η, this is because the number of bits that a user can transmit, depends on the MCS, as well as the number of PRBs allocated to that users. For example, if the system spectrum is 5MHz (i.e., 25 PRBs) and η is equal to 5 users then on average each of the scheduled η users will be allocated 5 PRBs (that is 25/5).

The multiplication term in equation 7.10 represents the probability of the combination $(n_0, ..., n_K)$, and the multinomial coefficient represents the number of distinct permutations within that combination. For example, if a system is defined with 2 MCSs (K=2) and the two active users (UE1 and UE2) are present in the system, i.e., n=2, then one of the possible combinations is $(n_0, n_1, n_2) = (0, 1, 1)$, now the multiplication term will give the probability of that combination, but there are distinct possibilities where UE1 and UE2 might be within that combination, mainly $(n_0, n_1, n_2) = (0, UE1, UE2)$ or $(n_0, n_1, n_2) = (0, UE2, UE1)$ and that's what the multinomial coefficient represents.

Now looking at the whole equation after explaining all the individual parts, it can be seen that it is a weighted average formula. Since each combination number of transmitted bits $\overline{TBS}(n_0, ..., n_K)$ is multiplied with its probability and all the combinations are summed together. The final results are the average number of transmitted bits of state n.

7.2 LTE Downlink Scheduler Modeling

This section discusses the analytical modeling of the LTE downlink scheduler using the general analytical model explained earlier in section 7.1. The modeling is done in two stages: the first stage models the LTE scheduler with a single class, where no QoS differentiation is present. The second stage models the scheduler with QoS differentiation and using two nonGBR QoS classes. The downlink LTE scheduler as described earlier consists of two schedulers: a Time Domain Scheduler (TDS) and a Frequency Domain Scheduler (FDS). The FDS scheduler within this thesis work is a Round Robin scheduler that distributes the frequency resources (i.e., PRBs) equally over the highest η TD priority metric nonGBR users.

7.2.1 Single Class Model

With this model all users use the same traffic model, hence no QoS differentiation is present. The users generate infinite elastic ON/OFF traffic represented by an ON period file size $\overline{X_{on}}$ and an OFF period of waiting time represented by $\overline{T_{off}}$. Assuming that N users are present in the system then the model is the same CTMC model explained earlier in section 7.1 with arrival rate λ (see equation 7.1) and a departure rate of $\mu(n)$ (see equation 7.9).

$\mu(n)$ depends on the TD scheduling discipline since it is inherently dependent on $\overline{TBS}(n)$. Looking back at equation 7.12, it can be seen that the TDS is reflected in $X_{k,i}$. Where $X_{k,i}$ is chosen to be 0 or 1 depending on the time domain scheduler. Three different TDS schedulers are modeled in this thesis: BET, OSA and MaxT.

As a generalization, equation 7.11 can be rewritten in a more generic form that can incorporate all of the three TD schedulers as:

$$\overline{TBS}(n_0,...,n_K) = \sum_{i=[i_1,...,i_\eta]} TBS_i(\eta) \qquad (7.13)$$

with

$$\eta = min[n - n_0, \psi] \qquad (7.14)$$

where $[i_1,...,i_\eta]$ represents the index of the chosen η users out of the n active users considered for scheduling within a TTI, and ψ is the number of scheduled users by the FDS scheduler. Obviously the choice of the η users is determined by the TD scheduler.

Now, substituting equation 7.13 in equation 7.9, the generic departure rate $\mu(n)$ will be expressed as:

$$\mu(n) = \frac{1}{\overline{X_{on}} \cdot TTI} \sum_{\substack{(n_0,...,n_K)=(0,...,0)| \\ n_0+...+n_K=0 \\ n_0 \neq n}}^{(n,...,n)} n! \left[\sum_{i=[i_1,...,i_\eta]} TBS_i(\eta) \right] \left(\prod_{k=0}^{K} \frac{P_k^{n_k}}{n_k!} \right) \qquad (7.15)$$

Once all departure rates have been calculated for every state then the Markov chain steady state probability can be calculated as well as the average file download time using the techniques explained earlier (by using equation 7.6 and 7.3).

In order to model the different TD schedulers, the procedure (scheduler dependent) on how to choose η users out of the n active users has to be explained. For simplicity, the MaxT scheduler procedure is explained first. According to the definition of the MaxT scheduler (section 6.2.1) only the users with the best channel conditions are served, i.e., in every TTI the n active users are prioritized based on their channel conditions and then only the highest η users are scheduled. Now relating this to the analytical model the η users in the highest MCS are considered in the scheduling and represent the i user indices ($[i_1,...,i_\eta]$). This can be seen in Figure 7.2.

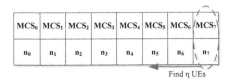

Figure 7.2: MaxT scheduling of users (example with 7 MCSs)

The reason why the MaxT is explained first is the fact that it only depends on the instantaneous channel conditions (i.e., MCSs). This makes the choice of the η users rather straight forward by only choosing the ones with the highest MCSs. In contrast to other scheduler disciplines like BET or OSA, where the choice of the η users does not only depend on the channel conditions but also on the accumulated sent throughput in the past. This makes the choice rather difficult, as there is a memory aspect in the decision which contradicts one of the basic principles of the Markov chain, that is the *memoryless* property.

In order to overcome the above mentioned problem, i.e., memory dependency, some work around is required in the analytical model. This can be done by approximating and emulating the behavior of the schedulers without actually dealing with the memory aspect. For example, the BET scheduler prioritizes the users based on their accumulated throughput from the past as described in equation 6.1. The main target of the BET scheduler is to equalize the users' throughputs, i.e., all users will get the same average throughput at the end. This can be approximated by choosing the η users from the MCSs that correspond to the average throughput. This can be seen in Figure 7.3.

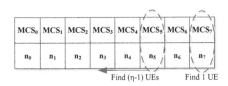

Figure 7.3: BET scheduling of users (example with 7 MCSs)

Figure 7.4 shows the MCSs static probability. This can be obtained for each specific scenario using simulations (with specific cell coverage, channel model and mobility model). The example figure was created using an eNodeB cell coverage of 375 km, with the channel model explained earlier in section 4.3.5 and both mobility models (RandomWay Point (RWP), and Random Direction (RD)).

Now, since the BET scheduler tries to let the users achieve the same average throughput, the analytical BET model chooses the η users from the MCS that achieves the average throughput. In the case of the RWP, it is MCS_5, whereas for the RD mobility model it is MCS_4. However, since the MCSs static probability (seen in Figure 7.4) shows that with a large probability a user can be in MCS_7 (50% for RWP, and above 30% for RD mobility model), one user out of the η chosen users is always chosen from MCS_7. The average MCS is chosen by roughly estimating the average throughput for each mobility model as follows:

$$AverageThroughput = \sum_{k=1}^{K} TBS_k \cdot P_k$$

where K represents the number of MCSs, TBS_k is the transport block size that can be transmitted when using MCS_k, and P_k is the static probability of MCS_k.

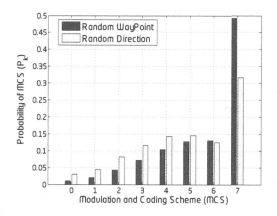

Figure 7.4: MCSs static probability obtained from simulations

The OSA scheduler has the same memory dependency problem similar to the BET scheduler. Thus, a similar approximation is required in order to overcome this problem, so as to emulate the OSA behavior. The OSA scheduler gives higher probability to users with better channel conditions. This can be seen in equation 6.5, where a normalized average channel condition factor in considered in the denominator of the time domain priority factor of the OSA scheduler.

The emulation of the OSA scheduler, i.e. the choice of the η users is shown in Figure 7.5. The figure shows that a higher average MCS is chosen (compared to the BET scheduler) due to the fact that the OSA scheduler prefers users with better channel conditions.

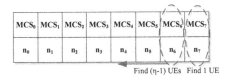

Figure 7.5: OSA scheduling of users (example with 7 MCSs)

7.2.2 Single Class Model Results

In this subsection, the single class analytical model is validated by comparing its results with simulation results. The analytical model is much faster in obtaining the results compared to simulations. The analytical model takes about 5 minutes to solve a scenario (with about 10 users), whereas, simulating the same scenario can take more than 5 hours (with 95% confidence interval, and 10 simulation seeds). The analytical model is implemented using *MATLAB*. The validation of the single class model is performed by checking different sensitivity parameters such as traffic model parameters and user constellations, i.e., different number of users. Table 7.2 and 7.3 show the configuration parameters and scenarios.

General parameter	(Value
Bandwidth (# PRBs)	5 MHz (i.e., 25 PRBs)
Number of users	10 UEs and 20 UEs
Mobility model	Random Way Point (RWP) with 120 km/h (The Random Direction (RD) is used for comparison in analysis 5)
Channel model	described in section 4.3.5
MCSs probability	Figure 7.4
DL Radio Schedulers	MaxT, BET, and OSA
Traffic model	FTP with different IATs and file sizes
Simulation run time	8000 seconds
Number of Simulation seeds	10 seeds; simulations with 95% confidence interval

Table 7.2: Single class validation general parameters

Analysis	TDS	(# of UEs)	FTP file size	FTP IAT
Analysis1	MaxT	10 UEs and 20 UEs	constant 5 MByte, 10 MByte, and 20 MByte	uniform (0, 30) seconds, uniform (15, 45) seconds, uniform (30, 60) seconds, and uniform (45, 75) seconds
Analysis2	BET	10 UEs and 20 UEs	constant 5 MByte, 10 MByte, and 20 MByte	uniform (0, 30) seconds, uniform (15, 45) seconds, uniform (30, 60) seconds, and uniform (45, 75) seconds
Analysis3	MaxT	10 UEs	negative exponential 5 MByte	neg. exp. (15) seconds, neg. exp. (30) seconds, neg. exp. (45) seconds, and neg. exp. (60) seconds
Analysis4	OSA	10 UEs	constant 5 MByte, 10 MByte, and 20 MByte	uniform (0, 30) seconds, uniform (15, 45) seconds, uniform (30, 60) seconds, and uniform (45, 75) seconds
Analysis5	BET (RD)	10 UEs	constant 5 MByte, 10 MByte, and 20 MByte	uniform (0, 30) seconds, uniform (15, 45) seconds, uniform (30, 60) seconds, and uniform (45, 75) seconds

Table 7.3: Single class validation scenarios

7.2.2.1 Analysis 1 - MaxT

In this section, the MaxT scheduler analytical model results are compared with the simulation ones. The analytical model is investigated under different sensitivity analyses. First of all, the MaxT model is validated against changing the total number of users, mainly two cases: 10 and 20 users. Then within each of these two cases, different FTP traffic model parameters are used. At the beginning the FTP file size is changed from a small file size (5MByte), over a medium file size (10MByte) to a larger file size (20 MByte). Each of these FTP file sizes are combined with different file inter-arrival times that are uniformly distributed with mean: 15, 30, 45, and 60 seconds. The is done to check the analytical model sensitivity against different traffic loads, where a mean of 15 seconds inter-arrival time represents a highly loaded situation when compared to a scenario with a 60 seconds mean file inter-arrival time.

Figure 7.6 shows the average file download time results comparison between the analytical model and simulations for the 10 UEs scenarios. The solid lines represent the analytical results and the dotted lines represent the simulation results (Table A.2 shows the confidence interval of the simulation results). The results show three different curves representing the three different FTP file sizes (5MB, 10MB, and 15MB). The x-axis represents the different traffic loads, or in other words the different FTP file inter-arrival rates (15, 30, 45, and 60 seconds).

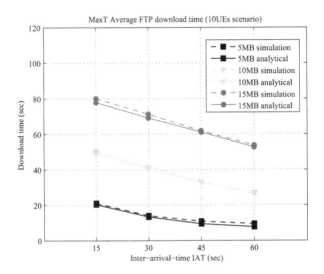

Figure 7.6: MaxT 10UEs scenario - average FTP download time

The results show that the analytical model results match the simulation results. The results prove that the MaxT analytical model is not sensitive against different traffic loads, i.e., different combinations of file sizes and IATs. Figure 7.7 shows the result comparison with the 20 users scenario. The analytical model still achieves accurate results compared to the simulation (Table A.3 shows the confidence interval of the simulation results) following the same results trend. However, it can be seen that when the traffic model goes to a larger FTP file sizes, a small gap between the analytical and simulation results starts appearing. The reason behind this gap is the fact that the system is highly loaded in these scenarios due to the high number of users (20UEs) and the large file size (15MByte), and as a result the number of samples in the FTP average file download time becomes smaller (fixed 8000 seconds simulation duration) because it takes much larger download time to finish a 15MByte file than the 5MByte case.

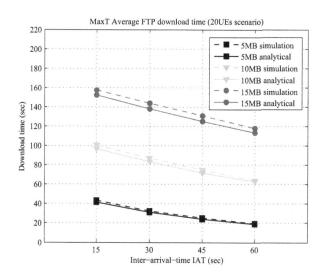

Figure 7.7: MaxT 20UEs scenario - average FTP download time

The Markov chain steady state probability π comparison between the analytical and simulation results for the 10 UEs and the 20 UEs scenarios can be seen in Figure 7.8. The results show that the steady state probability of the analytical model matches the simulation results.

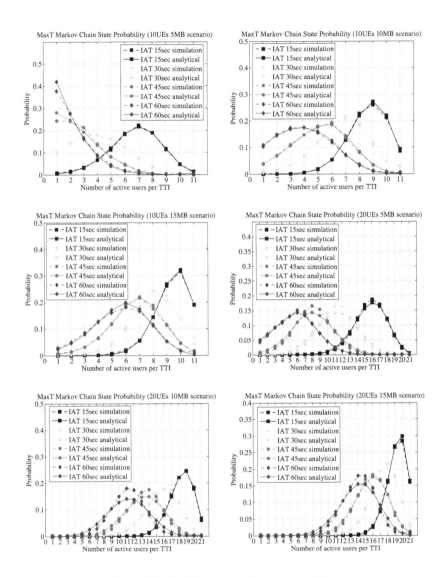

Figure 7.8: MaxT Markov chain state probability

7.2.2.2 Analysis 2 - BET

Similar to the MaxT scheduler, the BET analytical model results are compared against the simulation results. Several scenarios are investigated with different user numbers and different FTP traffic model parameters (Table 7.3).

Figure 7.9 shows the average file download time result comparison between the analytical model and simulations for the 10 UEs scenario. The solid lines represent the analytical results and the dotted lines represent the simulation results (Table A.4 shows the confidence interval of the simulation results). The results show three different curves representing the three different FTP file sizes (5MB, 10MB, and 15MB). The x-axis represents the different traffic load, or in other words the different FTP file inter-arrival rates (15, 30, 45, and 60 seconds).

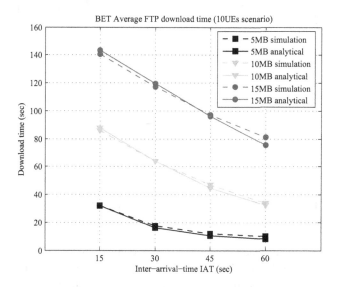

Figure 7.9: BET 10UEs scenario - average FTP download time

It can be seen from the results that the analytical model provides very close results to the simulation results. Although, an approximation for the BET scheduler behavior is used in the analytical model, the results confirm that the approximation used is a valid assumption and that the results match the simulation outcome. The 20 UEs scenario results can be seen in Figure 7.10 (Table A.5 shows the confidence interval of the simulation results). The results confirm that even with increasing the total number of users from 10 UEs to 20 UEs, the analytical model is still able to predict the average FTP download time and its trend when changing the FTP traffic parameters. Similar to the FTP results, a gap between the analytical and the simulation results starts appearing when increasing the load of the system especially in the overloaded scenario of 20 UEs with 15MB file size and 15 seconds average file inter-arrival time.

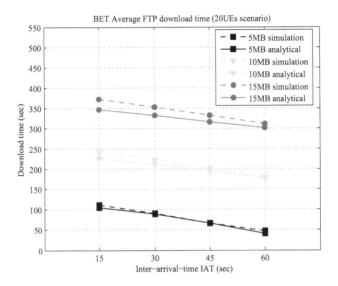

Figure 7.10: BET 20UEs scenario - average FTP download time

The Markov chain steady state probability π comparison between the analytical and simulation results for the 10 UEs and the 20 UEs scenario can be seen in Figure 7.11. The results show that the steady state probability of the analytical model matches the simulation results.

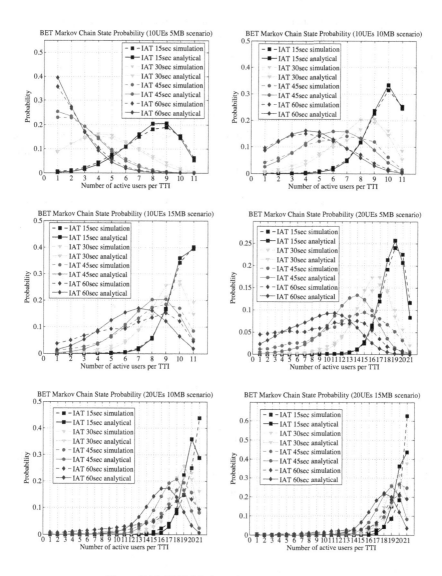

Figure 7.11: BET Markov chain state probability

7.2.2.3 Analysis 3 - Sensitivity Analysis

The intention of this scenario is to investigate the model sensitivity against using other distributions for the traffic model parameters. Instead of using a constant file size as in the previous two analyses, in this analysis, a negative exponential distribution is used for generating the file size, which is combined with several negative exponentially distributed inter-arrival times. Figure 7.12 shows the results of analysis 3 (Table A.6 shows the confidence interval of the simulation results). The left side figure, shows the average file download time. It can be seen, that although negative exponential distributions were used to generate the file size and the inter-arrival time, the model is quite insensitive to the change, and the results still match the results obtained from simulations.

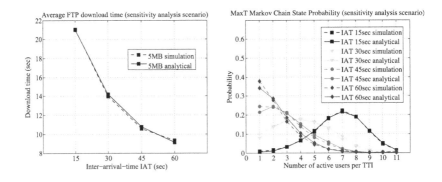

Figure 7.12: MaxT sensitivity analysis results

The Markov chain steady state probability π results can be seen in right side of Figure 7.12. The results show, that the steady state probability of the analytical model matches the simulations results. Similar conclusions regarding the model insensitivity were also described in [DBMC10]. There, it was shown that: *the average performance parameters are insensitive to the distribution of ON and OFF periods*.

7.2.2.4 Analysis 4 - OSA

The OSA analytical model results are compared against the simulation results. Several scenarios are investigated with different total number of users and different FTP traffic model parameters (Table 7.3).

Figure 7.13 shows the average file download time results comparison between the analytical model and simulations for the 10 UEs scenario. The solid lines represent the analytical results and the dotted lines represent the simulation results (Table A.7 shows the confidence interval of the simulation results). The results show three different curves representing the three different FTP file sizes (5MB, 10MB, and 15MB). The x-axis represents the different traffic load, or in other words the different FTP file inter-arrival rates (15, 30, 45, and 60 seconds).

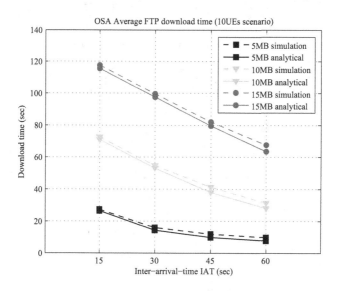

Figure 7.13: OSA 10UEs scenario - average FTP download time

It can be seen from the results that the analytical model provides very close results to the simulation results. Although, an approximation for the OSA scheduler behavior is used in the analytical model, the results confirm that the approximation used is a valid assumption and that the results match the simulation outcome.

The Markov chain steady state probability π comparison between the analytical and simulation results for the 10 UEs scenario can be seen in Figure 7.14. The results show that the steady state probability of the analytical model matches the simulations results.

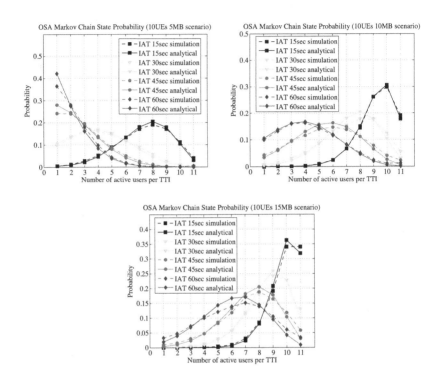

Figure 7.14: OSA Markov chain state probability

7.2.2.5 Analysis 5 - BET with Random Direction (RD)

In this section, the BET scheduler analytical model is analyzed using a different mobility model, that is the Random Direction (RD). The BET RD analytical model results are compared against the simulation results, for the several investigated scenarios: scenarios with different total number of users and different FTP traffic model parameters (Table 7.3). Figure 7.15 shows the average file download time results comparison. The solid lines represent the analytical results and the dotted lines represent the simulation results (Table A.8 shows the confidence interval of the simulation results). The figure shows the download times for the three FTP file sizes (5MB, 10MB, and 15MB) in combination with the different FTP file inter-arrival rates (15, 30, 45, and 60 seconds).

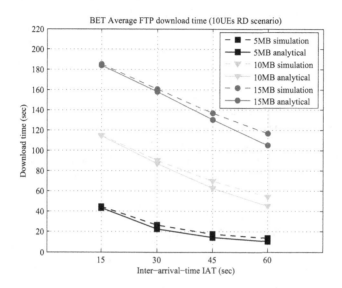

Figure 7.15: BET RD 10UEs scenario - average FTP download time

The results show that the FTP download times are increased compared to analysis 2 (Figure 7.9), this is because in analysis 2 the RWP mobility model is used, which tends to distribute the users density around the center of the eNodeB, which increases the probability of having a good channel condition. Thus, the users will have better channel conditions and a higher spectral efficiency which explains the faster FTP file downloads. In analysis 5, the RD mobility model uniformly distributes the users density within the cell, which increases the probability of being in a bad channel condition (see Figure 7.4), thus the spectral efficiency is reduced which will lead to slower FTP file downloads.

Nevertheless, the results show that the BET analytical model provides close results to the simulation results, in spite of changing the mobility model in this analysis.

7.2.3 Two-Dimensional Model

With this section, the single class model is extended to support two traffic classes. Hence, QoS differentiation is possible between these two traffic classes. Two infinite elastic ON/OFF traffic models can be supported in this model which are represented by $\overline{X_{1on}}$ and $\overline{X_{2on}}$ as the average file size for traffic model 1 and traffic model 2 respectively; and $\overline{t_{1off}}$ and $\overline{t_{2off}}$ as the average OFF period for traffic model 1 and traffic model 2 respectively.

Assuming a total N (N1+N2) users are present in the system, with N1 users using traffic model 1 (i.e., class1) and N2 users using traffic model 2 (i.e., class2), then the model is a 2D CTMC model with state (i,j), with i representing the number of active users in class1 and j representing the number of active users in class2. The 2D Markov chain has two arrival rates λ_1 and λ_2, and two departure rates of $\mu_1(i,j)$ and $\mu_2(i,j)$. Figure 7.16 shows the 2D Markov chain.

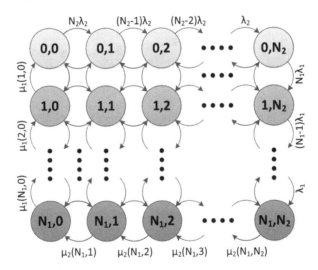

Figure 7.16: Two-dimensional Markov chain

The arrival rates λ_1 and λ_2 are calculated as follows:

$$\lambda_1 = \frac{1}{\overline{t_{1off}}} \tag{7.16}$$

$$\lambda_2 = \frac{1}{\overline{t_{2off}}} \tag{7.17}$$

The 2D Markov chain departure rates ($\mu_1(i,j)$ and $\mu_2(i,j)$) depend on the TD scheduler type, and are calculated as follows:

$$\mu_1(i,j) = \frac{\overline{TBS1}(i,j)}{\overline{X_{1on}} \cdot TTI} \tag{7.18}$$

$$\mu_2(i,j) = \frac{\overline{TBS2}(i,j)}{\overline{X_{2on}} \cdot TTI} \tag{7.19}$$

where, $\overline{TBS1}(i,j)$ represents the average data sent for all served users in class1 under the Markov chain (i,j), i.e., when the number of users of class1 are i and j in class2. $\overline{TBS2}(i,j)$ is the average data sent for all served users in class2 in state (i,j). $\overline{TBS1}(i,j)$ and $\overline{TBS2}(i,j)$ are calculated as follows:

$$\overline{TBS1}(i,j) = \sum_{\substack{(i_0,\ldots,i_K,j_0,\ldots,j_K)=(0,\ldots,0)| \\ i_0+\ldots+i_K=i \\ j_0+\ldots+j_K=j \\ i_0 \neq i \text{ with } j_0 \neq j}}^{(i,\ldots,i,j,\ldots,j)} i!\,j!\,\overline{TBS1}(i_0,\ldots,i_K,j_0,\ldots,j_K) \left[\prod_{k=0}^{K} \frac{P_k^{i_k} P_k^{j_k}}{i_k!\,j_k!} \right] \tag{7.20}$$

$$\overline{TBS2}(i,j) = \sum_{\substack{(i_0,\ldots,i_K,j_0,\ldots,j_K)=(0,\ldots,0)| \\ i_0+\ldots+i_K=i \\ j_0+\ldots+j_K=j \\ i_0 \neq i \text{ with } j_0 \neq j}}^{(i,\ldots,i,j,\ldots,j)} i!\,j!\,\overline{TBS2}(i_0,\ldots,i_K,j_0,\ldots,j_K) \left[\prod_{k=0}^{K} \frac{P_k^{i_k} P_k^{j_k}}{i_k!\,j_k!} \right] \tag{7.21}$$

where, $\overline{TBS1}(i_0,\ldots,i_K,j_0,\ldots,j_K)$ is the total data sent of the served class1 users under the specific combination $(i_0,\ldots,i_K,j_0,\ldots,j_K)$. Where, K is the total number of MCSs used. Equation 7.20, shows that the combinations space is now doubled $((i_0,\ldots,i_K,j_0,\ldots,j_K))$ compared to the single class model. This is because, all the possible combinations, where the users of class1 can be in the MCSs vector in combination with the second class, have to be covered. $\overline{TBS1}(i_0,\ldots,i_K,j_0,\ldots,j_K)$ is calculated as follows:

$$\overline{TBS1}(i_0,\ldots,i_K,j_0,\ldots,j_K) = \sum_{r=[r_1,\ldots,r_{\delta 1}]} TBS_r(\eta) \tag{7.22}$$

where, r is a vector representing the indices of the served users in class1 with $r_{\delta 1}$ being the number of users served in class1. $\overline{TBS2}(i_0,\ldots,i_K,j_0,\ldots,j_K)$ can be calculated similarly to $\overline{TBS1}(i_0,\ldots,i_K,j_0,\ldots,j_K)$. The total number of served users per TTI (i.e., η) is the sum of the served users in the two classes: $\eta = r_{\delta 1} + r_{\delta 2}$.

7.2.3.1 2D TDS Modeling

In order to model the different TD schedulers within the 2D analytical model, a scheduler dependent procedure on how to choose the η users out of the n active ones has to be devised. For simplicity, the w-MaxT scheduler is chosen as the time domain scheduler to explain the η users selection process. Notice, that the weighted version of the MaxT scheduler is chosen because the model supports two different traffic classes and the scheduler differentiates between the two class to enforce QoS differentiation. According to the definition of the w-MaxT scheduler (explained earlier in section 6.4.1.2), only the users with the best weighted channel conditions are served, i.e., every TTI the (i+j) active users are prioritized based on their channel conditions multiplied by the class weight factor and then only the highest η users are scheduled. The highest η users can consist of both traffic classes and that is why it is differentiated into two different sub-groups ($\delta 1$ and $\delta 2$). Each of these groups represents one of the traffic classes.

For the w-MaxT scheduler, since each MCS has a predefined target SINR value, that represents the lowest SINR value required to support this MCS with 10% BLER, then multiplying this target SINR with the scheduler weight W_{QoS_j} (2 for class1 and 1 for class2) and sorting them in order, in correspondence to their values from the highest value to the lowest value will lead to the prioritized candidate list for the w-MaxT (including the W_{QoS_j} wieghts), as follows:

$$\text{w-MaxT} = (i_7, i_6, i_5, i_4, i_3, i_2, i_1, j_7, j_6, j_5, j_4, j_3, j_2, j_1)$$

Similarly, a procedure for choosing the η users for the w-BET and OSA scheduler can be deduced. It was explained earlier, that for schedulers similar to BET and OSA, with memory characteristics, some approximation is required to emulate the behavior of these schedulers and to overcome the memory problem. The approximation used to model the w-BET and OSA scheduler is similar to the one used earlier for the single class scheduler. The users are chosen from the MCSs that correspond to the average throughput, while taking into consideration the additional weight W_{QoS_j} (e.g., 2 for class1 and 1 for class2) used to differentiate between the two classes. Thus, the prioritized candidate list for the w-BET and OSA scheduler will be:

$$\text{w-BET} = (i_5, i_4, j_5, j_4, i_3, i_2, j_3, j_2, i_1, j_1, i_6, j_6, i_7, j_7)$$

$$\text{OSA} = (i_6, j_6, i_5, i_4, j_5, j_4, i_3, i_2, j_3, j_2, i_1, j_1, i_7, j_7)$$

7.2.3.2 2D Performance Analysis

Once the departure rates are calculated, the steady state probabilities can be calculated using the equation 7.2 described earlier. The generator matrix **Q** has to be populated with the transition rates. In order to do that, the 2D Markov chain shown in Figure 7.16 can be redrawn as a one dimensional chain with transitions across several states as shown in Figure 7.17.

Figure 7.17: 2D Markov chain represented in a single chain

A mapping algorithm is required to map the Markov chain state transitions of the 2D Markov chain into the generator matrix **Q**. An example of such a mapping can be seen in Figure 7.18.

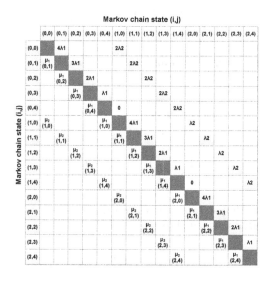

Markov chain state (i,j)

	(0,0)	(0,1)	(0,2)	(0,3)	(0,4)	(1,0)	(1,1)	(1,2)	(1,3)	(1,4)	(2,0)	(2,1)	(2,2)	(2,3)	(2,4)
(0,0)		$4\Lambda_1$				$2\Lambda_2$									
(0,1)	μ_1(0,1)		$3\Lambda_1$				$2\Lambda_2$								
(0,2)		μ_1(0,2)		$2\Lambda_1$				$2\Lambda_2$							
(0,3)			μ_1(0,3)		Λ_1				$2\Lambda_2$						
(0,4)				μ_1(0,4)		0				$2\Lambda_2$					
(1,0)	μ_2(1,0)					μ_1(1,0)	$4\Lambda_1$				Λ_2				
(1,1)		μ_2(1,1)				μ_1(1,1)		$3\Lambda_1$				Λ_2			
(1,2)			μ_2(1,2)				μ_1(1,2)		$2\Lambda_1$				Λ_2		
(1,3)				μ_2(1,3)				μ_1(1,3)		Λ_1				Λ_2	
(1,4)					μ_2(1,4)				μ_1(1,4)		0				Λ_2
(2,0)						μ_2(2,0)					μ_1(2,0)	$4\Lambda_1$			
(2,1)							μ_2(2,1)				μ_1(2,1)		$3\Lambda_1$		
(2,2)								μ_2(2,2)				μ_1(2,2)		$2\Lambda_1$	
(2,3)									μ_2(2,3)				μ_1(2,3)		Λ_1
(2,4)										μ_2(2,4)				μ_1(2,4)	

Markov chain state (i,j)

Figure 7.18: Example Q mapping with N1=2 and N2=4

The diagonal cells in the Q matrix (highlighted with gray in Figure 7.18) is the state self transition. According to [Kle76], the sum of the transition rates of each state should equal to zero, so as to create equilibrium. Thus, the value of the dark boxes is equal to:

$$Q(i,i) = - \sum_{\substack{\text{all } j \mid \\ j \neq i}} Q(i,j) \tag{7.23}$$

Once the Markov chain steady state probabilities have been calculated, the 2D model performance analysis can be evaluated. This is done in a way similar to the single class model (see section 7.1.1). First of all, the average number of active users in the system for each class $\overline{Q1}$ and $\overline{Q2}$ is calculated. As $\overline{Q1}$ and $\overline{Q2}$ are the mean number of users and $\pi(i,j)$ is the probability of every state, i.e. probability of having i active users in class1 and j active users in class2, then the average number of active users per class is:

$$\overline{Q1} = \sum_{i=0}^{N1} \sum_{j=0}^{N2} i\pi(i,j) \tag{7.24}$$

$$\overline{Q2} = \sum_{i=0}^{N1} \sum_{j=0}^{N2} j\pi(i,j) \tag{7.25}$$

Next, the mean number of departures by unit time $\overline{D1}$ and $\overline{D2}$ are calculated as follows:

$$\overline{D1} = \sum_{i=0}^{N1} \sum_{j=0}^{N2} \mu_1(i,j)\pi(i,j) \tag{7.26}$$

$$\overline{D2} = \sum_{i=0}^{N1} \sum_{j=0}^{N2} \mu_2(i,j)\pi(i,j) \tag{7.27}$$

And finally, according to Little's law [Ste11], the average ON duration, i.e. the average file download time per class is:

$$\overline{t_{1on}} = \frac{\overline{Q1}}{\overline{D1}} \tag{7.28}$$

$$\overline{t_{2on}} = \frac{\overline{Q2}}{\overline{D2}} \tag{7.29}$$

7.2.4 Two-Dimensional Model Results

The validation is performed by comparing the 2-D analytical model results against simulation results. Table 7.4 shows the general parameters used for both the simulations and the analytical model. On the other hand, Table 7.5 shows investigated scenarios parameters and configurations.

General parameter	Value
Bandwidth (# PRBs)	5 MHz (i.e., 25 PRBs)
Class weight	W_{QoS_j}=2 for class1, and 1 for class2
Mobility model	Random Way Point (RWP) with 120 km/h
MCSs probability	Figure 7.4
DL Radio Schedulers	OSA, w-MaxT and w-BET
Traffic model	FTP with different IATs and file sizes
Simulation run time	8000 seconds
Number of Simulation seeds	5 seeds; simulations with 95% confidence interval

Table 7.4: 2-D model validation general parameters

Analysis	TDS	C1 UEs	C2 UEs	C1 file size	C2 file size	C1/2 IAT
Analysis1	w-MaxT	3 UEs	6 UEs	constant 5 MByte	constant 10 MByte	uniform (0, 30) s, uniform (15, 45) s, uniform (30, 60) s, uniform (45, 75) s
Analysis2	w-MaxT	3 UEs	6 UEs	constant 10 MByte	constant 5 MByte	uniform (0, 30) s, uniform (15, 45) s, uniform (30, 60) s, uniform (45, 75) s
Analysis3	w-BET	3 UEs	6 UEs	constant 5 MByte	constant 10 MByte	uniform (0, 30) s, uniform (15, 45) s, uniform (30, 60) s, uniform (45, 75) s
Analysis4	w-BET	6 UEs	3 UEs	constant 10 MByte	constant 5 MByte	uniform (0, 30) s, uniform (15, 45) s, uniform (30, 60) s, uniform (45, 75) s
Analysis5	OSA	3 UEs	6 UEs	constant 5 MByte	constant 10 MByte	uniform (0, 30) s, uniform (15, 45) s, uniform (30, 60) s, uniform (45, 75) s

Table 7.5: 2-D model validation scenarios

7.2.4.1 Analysis - w-MaxT

The two-dimensional w-MaxT model is validated within this section. The w-MaxT model is tested with two different analysis scenarios, each with different traffic parameters. In analysis1, the FTP file size of class1 users is chosen to be a constant 5 MByte, whereas, the size of the class2 FTP traffic model is chosen to be a constant 10 MByte. Each of these file sizes is paired with several uniformly distributed file inter-arrival times, so as to emulate different traffic loads. In analysis2, the FTP file sizes are switched between the traffic classes, where class1 users are configured to generate constant 10 MByte FTP files, and class2 users generate constant 5 MByte FTP files. The average FTP file download times for both analysis1 and analysis2 are shown in Figure 7.19 and Figure 7.20 respectively.

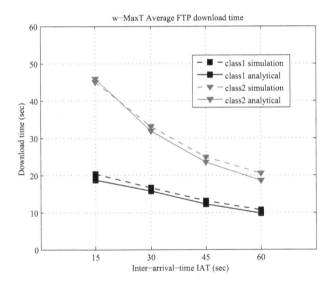

Figure 7.19: Analysis1 w-MaxT average FTP download time

The figures show that the w-MaxT model results match the simulation results (Table A.9 and Table A.10 show the confidence interval of the simulation results for analysis1 and analysis2 respectively). The results also prove that the w-MaxT analytical model is not sensitive against different traffic parameters, i.e., different combinations of file sizes and IATs.

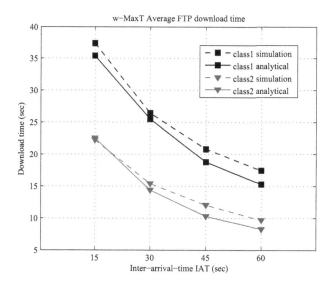

Figure 7.20: Analysis2 w-MaxT average FTP download time

The Markov chain state probability comparison is shown in Figure 7.21 and Figure 7.22, for both anaylsis1 and analysis2, respectively. It can be seen that each figure is divided into four smaller sub-figures, this is because of the two-dimensional Markov chain, i.e., two different classes. Each of the sub-figures represents a state of class1 (the i of the Markov chain state (i,j)). since, only 3 users are configured in class1, then i can have four different possibilities: from no active users (i.e., i=0), to all users in class1 are active (i.e., i=3). Then, the x-axis within each sub-figures represents the state of class 2 (the j of the Markov chain (i,j)). The different line curves shown in the sub-figures represent the different file inter-arrival scenarios.

The Markov chain state probability also strengthens the aforementioned conclusion, i.e., that the w-MaxT analytical model is a very good mathematical of the w-MaxT LTE time domain scheduler.

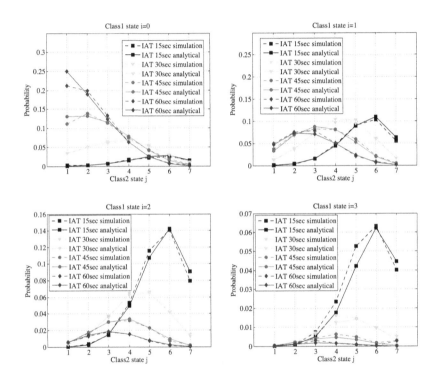

Figure 7.21: Analysis1 w-MaxT Markov chain state probability

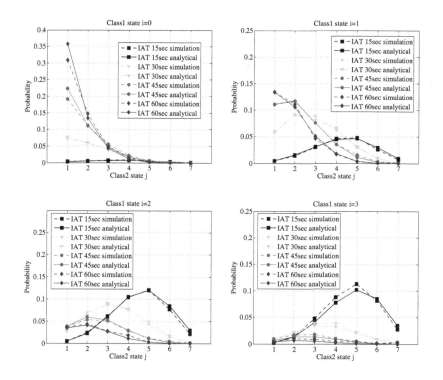

Figure 7.22: Analysis2 w-MaxT Markov chain state probability

7.2.4.2 Analysis - w-BET

The w-BET analytical model is validated against the simulation results in this section. The validation includes several scenarios with a sensitivity analysis of the
model parameters: against different traffic model parameters, e.g. FTP file size and
FTP file inter-arrival time, and against different users constellations. The analyses
are divided into two main categories as seen in Table 7.5: in analysis3, the number
of users in class1 and class2 is set to 3 and 6 respectively, whereas in analysis4,
the number of users in each class are exchanged to be 6 users in class1 and 3 users
in class2. Each of these analysis categories contains several sub-scenarios, to test
against several traffic loads.

Figure 7.23 shows the average FTP download time per class for both the analytical model and the simulation model results (Table A.11 shows the confidence
interval of the simulation results for analysis3).

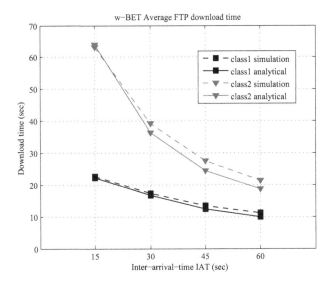

Figure 7.23: Analysis3 w-BET average FTP download time

The results show, that the analytical model results matches the simulation results. When the inter-arrival time of the FTP traffic model is increased, a gap
between the analytical and the simulations starts appearing. The reason behind the
gap is that when the inter-arrival time between the files increases, the system will

have a lower traffic load and the overall number of FTP downloads decreases since within the same simulation time period a smaller number of FTP files is generated. Since the analytical model focuses only on the MAC scheduler and does not model other layers and functionalities (e.g., TCP), when the traffic load decreases the TCP slow start effect increases which explains the gap between the simulations and the analytical results. However, the gap still represents a relative error of about 10% or less, which is an acceptable error.

The Markov chain steady state probability comparison between the analytical model and the simulation model is shown in Figure 7.24.

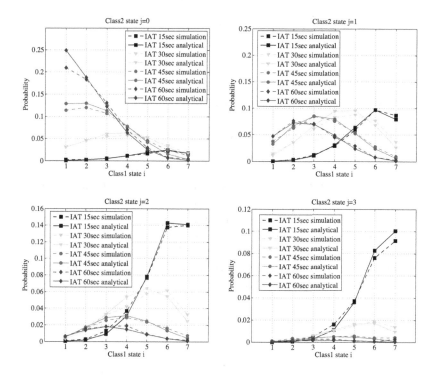

Figure 7.24: Analysis3 w-BET Markov chain state probability

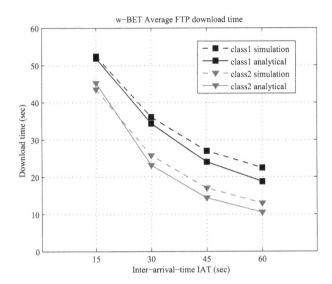

Figure 7.25: Analysis4 w-BET average FTP download time

Figure 7.25 shows the second analysis category average FTP download time (Table A.12 shows the confidence interval of the simulation results for analysis4). In this analysis, the user constellation is changed, i.e., the number of users in each class is changed (6 users in class1 and 3 users in class2). Again, several FTP parameters, i.e. traffic loads, are investigated. The results show that the w-BET analytical model still predicts the results accurately. The Markov chain steady state probability results are shown in Figure 7.26.

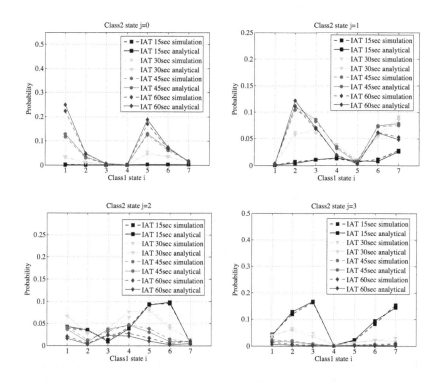

Figure 7.26: Analysis4 w-BET Markov chain state probability

7.2.4.3 Analysis - OSA

The OSA analytical model is validated against the simulation results in this section. The validation is done against simulations with different FTP file inter-arrival times. The scenario is configured with three users in class1 and six users in class2. Each of these categories contains several sub-scenarios to test against several traffic loads. Figure 7.27 shows the average FTP download time per class for both the analytical model and the simulation model results.

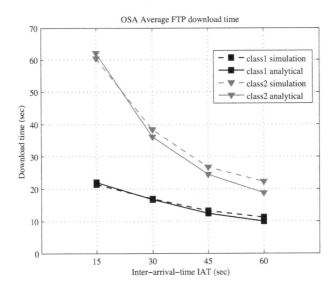

Figure 7.27: Analysis5 OSA average FTP download time

The results show that the analytical model results match the simulation results. Similar to the w-BET results, it can be observed that when the inter-arrival time of the FTP traffic model is increased a gap between the analytical and the simulations starts appearing. This reason behind the gap is again the effect of the TCP slow start, where it's effect will become more visible when the traffic load decreases. However, as stated earlier, the gap still represents a relative error of about 10% or less, which is an acceptable error margin.

7.3 Conclusion

The analytical modeling of the LTE radio scheduler is discussed and developed in this chapter. The analytical models are based on the Continuous Time Markov Chain model. Three different LTE time domain schedulers have been modeled in this chapter: Maximum Throughput (MaxT), Blind Equal Throughput (BET) and Optimized Service Aware (OSA). The analytical model is developed in two stages: in the first stage, no QoS differentiation was considered and only one traffic class is modeled; whereas in the next stage, a two-dimensional model is developed so as to model the QoS differentiations between two traffic classes.

The developed analytical models are compared against the simulation model and the result comparison proves that the analytical model results matches the simulation ones. The results comparison showed that in most cases the simulation results, i.e. the file download times, are often slightly higher than the analytical results. The reason behind this is the fact that the analytical model only models the radio scheduler, whereas, the simulation model includes the full protocol stack of all the nodes. In addition, the TCP slow start effect is not reflected in the analytical model, which is another reason why the simulation results are slightly higher than the analytical results. Nevertheless, the analytical models proposed in this thesis showed accurate results and thus they can be used as reliable tools to perform radio dimensioning and generate results in a very short time period.

8 Conclusions and Outlook

The work presented in this thesis focused on the optimization of the 3GPP Long Term Evolution (LTE) standard, with special focus on the LTE radio part. In addition, the work also introduced a futuristic look of wireless mobile networks by using network virtualization techniques to virtualize the infrastructure and let operators share the infrastructure and the spectrum. As a result a novel LTE wireless virtualization framework has been proposed, that achieves better spectral efficiency, flexibility and end-user performance.

The work involved the implementation and validation of a comprehensive LTE simulation model based on the OPNET simulator, according to the 3GPP specifications. The corresponding LTE E-UTRAN nodes (UEs, enodeBs and aGWs) with their respective protocols have been modeled and implemented with full details. Furthermore, an LTE downlink radio scheduler has been designed and developed. A realistic channel model is also implemented in the simulator so as to be able to perform detailed analysis and evaluations. In addition, several LTE radio scheduler analytical models have been developed and implemented in MATLAB. The simulation results of the OPNET simulation model are validated against the developed MATLAB analytical models.

The developed LTE simulation models have been used by several other industrial and European research projects, for example, it is used by Nokia Siemens Networks to study, investigate and analyze the LTE E-UTRAN performance. It has been used by the 4WARD European project as a proof of concept use case for applying network virtualization in mobile networks. Furthermore, the model is also being used to study the benefits of multi-path transmission of 3GPP LTE systems inter-connected with WLAN [ZZU+11]. Finally, the model is also used for scientific research and development by students for their master thesis (e.g., [Zah11], [Mar11], [Mei12]). On the other hand, the developed LTE scheduler analytical models can be used for fast radio dimensioning purposes. It provides a good tool to generate accurate results in a very short time (in the order of minutes for small scenarios).

The performance of different LTE radio schedulers on the end user performance and fairness were investigated and analyzed using both simulations and analytical tools. The simulation results showed that the Optimized Service Aware Scheduler (OSA) outperforms other schedulers and provides the right balance between spectral efficiency, as well as performance and fairness among the scheduled users. Another aspect of scheduling was investigated, that is the exploitation of the Guaranteed Bit Rate (GBR) services tolerance against static delays up to their QoS limit thresholds. It was shown that by doing so, for example delaying the VoIP user traffic intentionally up to a certain delay threshold, the overall system spectral efficiency was increased due to the better multiplexing gain, as well as the better spectral efficiency. In addition, the performance of other nonGBR services (like HTTP and FTP) were improved.

The advantages introduced by the LTE virtualization, based on spectrum sharing between different operators were studied and investigated within this work. An innovative wireless virtualization framework was proposed to virtualize the LTE system. The investigations showed that a better multiplexing gain due to spectrum sharing, as well as enhanced overall system utilization due to the full exploitation of the multi-user diversity gain can be achieved.

Furthermore, sharing the infrastructure of the LTE system leads to less equipment and thus reduces the power consumption, reducing the operators capital investment and providing flexibility into the operator's networks, where operators can shrink/expand and do changes to their virtual network on the fly very easily.

The developed OSA scheduler is proven to be a very attractive downlink scheduler, that provides good QoS guarantees for the different traffic services. In addition, the OSA scheduler is very simple, easy to implement and only requires small computations; all of these make the scheduler a very practical solution for real product deployments.

The analytical models developed in this thesis can serve as a basis for further extensions. Mainly, extending the models into more than two traffic classes, in order to provide a wider variety of service differentiation. The principle of GBR services can also be easily integrated into the analytical models, since they require a fixed amount of resources which can be modeled by subtracting them from the total resources and using the left resources for the nonGBR services. Additional models for other Time Domain Schedulers (TDS) flavors can also be derived from the models presented in this thesis work.

As for the LTE virtualization, this work sets a good starting point for future research. For example, cooperative spectrum sharing in a multi-cell scenario, where the interference management is considered or investigating an enhanced load estimation mechanism that can determine each virtual operators required bandwidth (i.e. PRBs) in a more accurate and dynamic way. In addition, investigations on the joint use of LTE load balancing and network virtualization can also be studied.

The OSA scheduler sets a good basis for the development of an uplink LTE radio scheduler that can provide QoS guarantees between services and efficiently use the uplink spectrum. Although this is not discussed in this thesis some work has already began in the designing and investigation of the LTE uplink scheduler, further details can be found in [MWZ+12a] [MWZ+12b] and [MWZ+12c]. Extensions of the analytical models towards the uplink scheduler are also the targeted subjects of the author's future work.

Appendix

A Appendix

A.1 Mobility Models

In this section the mobility models used in the simulator are explained. Two general mobility models are implemented: RandomWay Point (RWP) and Random Direction (RD) [AB08]. Both of these models relies on random processes to emulate the user movements and position within the cell.

The RWP first distributes the users within the cell, the initial positions of the users are chosen randomly within the cell. The user initial position $P1=(x_1,y_1)$ is chosen uniformly by choosing an x-position between the cell minimum and maximum x position, and similarly by choosing a y-position. Then each user will pick up randomly a destination point $P2=(x_2,y_2)$ and then starts moving with its velocity towards P2. Once the user reaches P2, it pauses for some time and then picks a new random position with the cell to move towards. This can be seen in Figure A.1(a).

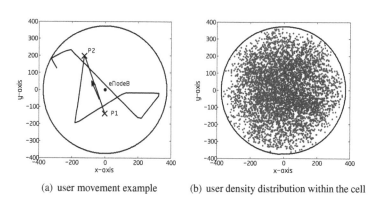

(a) user movement example   (b) user density distribution within the cell

Figure A.1: Random Way Point (RWP) mobility model

The RWP is a very simple and easy to implement mobility model. However, it suffers from a number of drawbacks, the most well known issue is the user density distribution within the cell, where after long simulation run is becomes non-uniform. The RWP tends to concentrate the users around the center of the region [AB08]. This can be seen in Figure A.1(b).

To overcome the non-uniform issue of the RWP, the Random direction (RD) mobility model was proposed. The RD model is very similar to the RWP with one exception, that is the user destinations. In contrast to the RWP, where the users destinations are randomly chosen with the whole cell, the RD chooses the users destinations points randomly on the cell boundaries. This can be seen in Figure A.2(a). In addition, Figure A.2(b) shows the users density distribution for the RD mobility model. It can be seen that the RD density distribution is uniform with the cell.

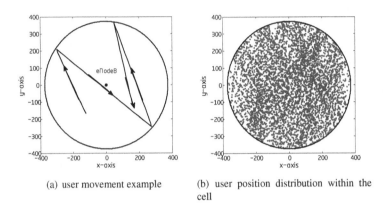

(a) user movement example   (b) user position distribution within the cell

Figure A.2: Random Direction (RD) mobility model

A.2 3GPP Transport Block Size

The full table can be found in [36.10a].

I_{TBS}	N_{PRB}									
	1	2	3	4	5	6	7	8	9	10
0	16	32	56	88	120	152	176	208	224	256
1	24	56	88	144	176	208	224	256	328	344
2	32	72	144	176	208	256	296	328	376	424
3	40	104	176	208	256	328	392	440	504	568
4	56	120	208	256	328	408	488	552	632	696
5	72	144	224	328	424	504	600	680	776	872
6	328	176	256	392	504	600	712	808	936	1032
7	104	224	328	472	584	712	840	968	1096	1224
8	120	256	392	536	680	808	968	1096	1256	1384
9	136	296	456	616	776	936	1096	1256	1416	1544
10	144	328	504	680	872	1032	1224	1384	1544	1736
11	176	376	584	776	1000	1192	1384	1608	1800	2024
12	208	440	680	904	1128	1352	1608	1800	2024	2280
13	224	488	744	1000	1256	1544	1800	2024	2280	2536
14	256	552	840	1128	1416	1736	1992	2280	2600	2856
15	280	600	904	1224	1544	1800	2152	2472	2728	3112
16	328	632	968	1288	1608	1928	2280	2600	2984	3240
17	336	696	1064	1416	1800	2152	2536	2856	3240	3624
18	376	776	1160	1544	1992	2344	2792	3112	3624	4008
19	408	840	1288	1736	2152	2600	2984	3496	3880	4264
20	440	904	1384	1864	2344	2792	3240	3752	4136	4584
21	488	1000	1480	1992	2472	2984	3496	4008	4584	4968
22	520	1064	1608	2152	2664	3240	3752	4264	4776	5352
23	552	1128	1736	2280	2856	3496	4008	4584	5160	5736
24	584	1192	1800	2408	2984	3624	4264	4968	5544	5992
25	616	1256	1864	2536	3112	3752	4392	5160	5736	6200
26	712	1480	2216	2984	3752	4392	5160	5992	6712	7480

Table A.1: 3GPP transport block size table (subset)

A.3 Simulation Results Confidence Interval

	15 sec	30 sec	45 sec	60 sec
5 MByte	0.16	0.39	0.28	0.46
10 MByte	0.23	0.46	0.24	0.61
15 MByte	0.48	0.49	0.20	0.58

Table A.2: Analysis 1 - MaxT 10 UEs simulation results confidence interval

	15 sec	30 sec	45 sec	60 sec
5 MByte	0.14	0.13	0.16	0.16
10 MByte	0.20	0.15	0.20	0.44
15 MByte	0.18	0.22	0.30	0.36

Table A.3: Analysis 1 - MaxT 20 UEs simulation results confidence interval

	15 sec	30 sec	45 sec	60 sec
5 MByte	0.51	0.39	0.31	0.33
10 MByte	0.77	0.73	1.37	1.14
15 MByte	1.46	1.00	2.20	4.12

Table A.4: Analysis 2 - BET 10 UEs simulation results confidence interval

	15 sec	30 sec	45 sec	60 sec
5 MByte	0.75	0.67	0.97	1.30
10 MByte	1.49	1.78	1.42	1.90
15 MByte	2.47	2.25	2.49	3.04

Table A.5: Analysis 2 - BET 20 UEs simulation results confidence interval

	15 sec	30 sec	45 sec	60 sec
5 MByte	0.53	0.35	0.13	0.27

Table A.6: Analysis 3 - BET sensitivity analysis simulation results confidence interval

	15 sec	30 sec	45 sec	60 sec
5 MByte	0.23	0.20	0.34	0.25
10 MByte	0.31	0.67	1.17	0.56
15 MByte	0.51	0.68	1.02	1.62

Table A.7: Analysis 4 - OSA simulation results confidence interval

	15 sec	30 sec	45 sec	60 sec
5 MByte	0.41	0.43	0.63	0.33
10 MByte	1.07	0.97	1.77	2.91
15 MByte	1.20	1.13	1.20	1.97

Table A.8: Analysis 5 - BET RD simulation results confidence interval

	15 sec	30 sec	45 sec	60 sec
Class1	0.72	0.66	0.48	0.81
Class2	1.94	1.27	1.58	1.83

Table A.9: Analysis 1 - w-MaxT simulation results confidence interval

	15 sec	30 sec	45 sec	60 sec
Class1	1.32	1.49	1.80	1.49
Class2	1.94	1.27	1.58	1.83

Table A.10: Analysis 2 - w-MaxT simulation results confidence interval

	15 sec	30 sec	45 sec	60 sec
Class1	0.49	0.45	0.53	0.73
Class2	2.03	1.38	1.24	1.45

Table A.11: Analysis 3 - w-BET simulation results confidence interval

	15 sec	30 sec	45 sec	60 sec
Class1	1.07	1.30	1.56	1.88
Class2	1.35	0.86	1.30	1.02

Table A.12: Analysis 4 - w-BET simulation results confidence interval

Bibliography

[25.04]   3GPP Technical Report TR 25.892. Feasibility Study for Orthogonal Fre-
            quency Division Multiplexing (OFDM) for UTRAN enhancement. Techni-
            cal Report version 6.0.0, 3rd Generation Partnership Project, June 2004.

[25.05]   3GPP Technical Report TR 25.913. Requirements for Evolved UTRA
            and UTRAN. Technical Report version 2.1.0., 3rd Generation Partnership
            Project, June 2005.

[25.06]   3GPP Technical Report TS 25.814. Physical layer aspects for Enhanced
            UTRA. Technical Report version 7.1.0, 3rd Generation Partnership Project,
            September 2006.

[36.10a]   3GPP Technical Report TS 36.213.   E-UTRA - Physical layer proce-
            dures. Technical Report version 9.3.0, 3rd Generation Partnership Project,
            September 2010.

[36.10b]   3GPP Technical Specification TS 36.322. Evolved Universal Terrestrial
            Radio Access (E-UTRA); Radio Link Control (RLC) protocol specifica-
            tion. Technical Report Version 10.0.0, 3rd Generation Partnership Project,
            December 2010.

[36.11a]   3GPP Technical Specification TS 36.300. Evolved Universal Terrestrial
            Radio Access (E-UTRA) and Evolved Universal Terrestrial Radio Access
            Network (E-UTRAN); Overall description; Stage 2. Technical Report Ver-
            sion 10.3.0, 3rd Generation Partnership Project, March 2011.

[36.11b]   3GPP Technical Specification TS 36.321. Evolved Universal Terrestrial Ra-
            dio Access (E-UTRA); Medium Access Control (MAC) protocol specifica-
            tion. Technical Report Version 10.2.0, 3rd Generation Partnership Project,
            June 2011.

[36.11c]   3GPP Technical Specification TS 36.323. Evolved Universal Terrestrial
            Radio Access (E-UTRA); Packet Data Convergence Protocol (PDCP) spec-
            ification. Technical Report Version 10.1.0, 3rd Generation Partnership
            Project, March 2011.

[3GP12]   3GPP. 3rd generation partnership project specification numbering.
            http://www.3gpp.org/Specification-Numbering ,
            last accessed on May 2012.

[4WAa]   4WARD. D-2.2 draft architectural framework.
            http://www.4ward-project.eu/index.php?s=Deliverables .
            last accessed on April 2012.

[4WAb]   4WARD. D-3.1.1 virtualization approach: Concept.
            http://www.4ward-project.eu/index.php?s=Deliverables .
            last accessed on April 2012.

[4WAc]   4WARD. D-4.2 in-network management concept.
            http://www.4ward-project.eu/index.php?s=Deliverables .
            last accessed on April 2012.

[4WAd]   4WARD. D-5.2.0 description of generic path mechanism.
            http://www.4ward-project.eu/index.php?s=Deliverables .
            last accessed on April 2012.

[4WAe]   4WARD. D-6.1 first netinf architecture description.
            http://www.4ward-project.eu/index.php?s=publications .
            last accessed on April 2012.

[4WAf]   4WARD. Fp7 european project. http://www.4ward-project.eu/ .
            last accessed on April 2012.

[AB08]   A. Alshanyour and U. Baroudi. Random and realistic mobility models im-
            pact on the performance of bypass-aodv routing protocol. In *Wireless Days,
            2008. WD '08. 1st IFIP*, pages 1 –5, nov. 2008.

[ABJS06]   R. Agrawal, R. Berry, Huang Jianwei, and V. Subramanian. Optimal
            scheduling for ofdma systems. signals, systems and computers. In *ACSSC
            '06*, Fortieth Asilomar Conference, 2006.

[ADF+09]   D. Astely, E. Dahlman, A. Furuskar, Y. Jading, M. Lindstrom, and S. Park-
            vall. Lte: the evolution of mobile broadband. *Communications Magazine,
            IEEE*, 47(4):44 –51, april 2009.

[Agi09]   Agilent. 3gpp long term evolution: System overview, product development,
            and test challenges. *Application Note*, June 2009.

[Agi11]   Agilent. Introducing lte-advanced. *Application Note*, March 2011.

[AKA10]   AKARI. New generation network architecture akari conceptual design (ver
            2.0). http://akari-project.nict.go.jp/eng/concept-design/AKARI_fulltext_e_
            preliminary_ver2.pdf , May 2010.

[AMVC07]   R. Agarwal, V. Majjigi, R. Vannithamby, and J. Cioffi. Efficient scheduling
            for heterogeneous services in ofdma downlink. In *IEEE Globecom*, Wash-
            ington D.C., 2007.

[Anr09]   Anritsu. Lte resource guide. *Anritsu Testing the FUTURE*, 2009.

[Asi]   AsiaFI. Asia future internet forum. http://www.asiafi.net/ .

[BAD08]   K. C. Beh, S. Armour, and A. Doufexi. Joint time-frequency domain pro-
           portional fair scheduler with harq for 3gpp lte systems. In *Vehicular Tech-
           nology Conference, 2008. VTC 2008-Fall. IEEE 68th*, pages 1 –5, sept.
           2008.

[BAS+05]   K. Brueninghaus, D. Astely, T. Salzer, S. Visuri, A. Alexiou, S. Karger,
           and G.-A. Seraji. Link performance models for system level simulations
           of broadband radio access systems. In *Personal, Indoor and Mobile Radio
           Communications, 2005. PIMRC 2005. IEEE 16th International Symposium
           on*, volume 4, pages 2306 –2311 Vol. 4, sept. 2005.

[BFH+06]   A. Bavier, N. Feamster, M. Huang, L. Peterson, and J. Rexford. In vini
           veritas: realistic and controlled network experimentation. In *Proceedings
           of the 2006 conference on Applications, technologies, architectures, and
           protocols for computer communications*, SIGCOMM '06, pages 3–14, New
           York, NY, USA, 2006. ACM.

[BMM+08]   S. Bhatia, M. Motiwala, W. Muhlbauer, V. Valancius, A. Bavier, N. Feam-
           ster, L. Peterson, and J. Rexford. Hosting virtual networks on commodity
           hardware. In *Tech. Rep. GT-CS-07-10*, Georgia Tech University, January
           2008.

[CBD02]   T. Camp, J. Boleng, and V. Davies. A survey of mobility models for ad
           hoc network research. *Wireless Communications and Mobile Computing*,
           2(5):483–502, 2002.

[Cha09]   D. Chantry. Mapping applications to the cloud. *MSDN library, http://
           msdn.microsoft.com/en-us/library/dd430340.aspx* , January 2009.

[Cis]   Cisco. Vn-link.
           http://www.cisco.com/en/US/solutions/collateral/ns340/ns517/ns224/
           ns892/ns894/white_paper_c11-525307_ps9902_Products_White_Paper.
           html .

[CW08]   L. M. Correia and K. Wuenstel. WP1 BIRD: Business Innovation, Regula-
           tion and Dissemination. In *ICT Mobile Summit (presentation)*, Stockholm,
           June 2008.

[CYG95]   C. N. Chuah, R. D. Yates, and D. J. Goodman. Integrated dynamic ra-
           dio resource management. In *IEEE 45th Vehicular Technology Conference*,
           volume 2, pages 584–588, Chicago, IL, USA, July 1995.

[Dah07]   E. Dahlman. *3G evolution: HSPA and LTE for mobile broadband*. Elec-
           tronics & Electrical. Elsevier Academic Press, 2007.

[DBMC10]   S. Doirieux, B. Baynat, M. Maqbool, and M. Coupechoux. An efficient
           analytical model for the dimensioning of wimax networks supporting multi-
           profile best effort traffic. *Computer Communications*, 33(10):1162 – 1179,
           2010.

[DMA03]   M. Dillinger, K. Madani, and N. Alonistioti. *Software defined radio: architectures, systems, and functions*. Wiley series in software radio. Wiley, 2003.

[EK06]   M. Einhaus and O. Klein. Performance evaluation of a basic ofdma scheduling algorithm for packet data transmissions. In *ISCC*, Cagliary, Italy, 2006.

[EKW08]   M. Einhaus, O. Klein, and B. Walke. Comparison of ofdma resource scheduling strategies with fair allocation of capacity. In *5th IEEE Consumer Communications and Networking Conference (CCNC 2008)*, Las Vegas, NV, January 2008.

[GEN]   GENI. Global Environment for Network Innovations. http://www.geni.net/ .

[GL08]   M. Gidlund and J.-C. Laneri. Scheduling algorithms for 3gpp long-term evolution systems: From a quality of service perspective. In *Spread Spectrum Techniques and Applications, 2008. ISSSTA '08. IEEE 10th International Symposium on*, pages 114 –117, aug. 2008.

[Hoa05]   J. Hoadley. Building future networks with mimo and ofdm. *http://connectedplanetonline.com/wireless/technology/mimo_ofdm_091905/* , September 2005.

[HSH+97]   S. Hämäläinen, P. Slanina, M. Hartman, A. Lappeteläinen, H. Holma, and O. Salonaho. A novel interface between link and system level simulations. In *Proc. of ACTS Mobile Communications Summit '97*, volume 2, pages 559–604. Aalborg, Denmark, October 1997.

[HT07]   H. Holma and A. Toskala. *WCDMA for UMTS: HSPA evolution and LTE*. Wiley, 2007.

[HT09]   H. Holma and A. Toskala. *LTE for UMTS: OFDMA and SC-FDMA based radio access*. Wiley, 2009.

[HUN86]   J.S. HUNTER. The exponentially weighted moving average. In *Jal Quality Technology*, volume 18, pages 203–210, 1986.

[IBM03]   IBM. Storage virtualization tutorial. http://www-03.ibm.com/systems/resources/systems_storage_software_ virtualization_tutorial_booklet1.pdf , 2003.

[IT09]   ITU-T. Recommendation g.114 (05/03). *One-way transmission time*, 2009.

[Kle76]   L. Kleinrock. *Queueing Systems: Theory*. Number Bd. 1 in A Wiley-Interscience publication. Wiley, 1976.

[KLZ09]   R. Kwan, C. Leung, and J. Zhang. Proportional fair multiuser scheduling in lte. *Signal Processing Letters, IEEE*, 16(6):461 –464, june 2009.

[KMC+00]   E. Kohler, R. Morris, B. Chen, J. Jahnotti, and M. F. Kasshoek. The click modular router. In *ACM Transaction on Computer Systems*, vol. 18, no- 3, 2000.

[KPK⁺08a]   P. Kela, J. Puttonen, N. Kolehmainen, T. Ristaniemi, T. Henttonen, and M. Moisio. Dynamic packet scheduling performance in utra long term evolution downlink. In *Wireless Pervasive Computing, 2008. ISWPC 2008. 3rd International Symposium on*, pages 308–313, may 2008.

[KPK⁺08b]   P. Kela, J. Puttonen, N. Kolehmainen, T. Ristaniemi, T. Henttonen, and M. Moisio. Dynamic packet scheduling performance in utra long term evolution downlink. In *Wireless Pervasive Computing, 2008. ISWPC 2008. 3rd International Symposium on*, pages 308–313, may 2008.

[KSK⁺08]   A. Kopke, M. Swigulski, K.Wessel, D. Willkomm, P.T. K. Haneveld, T. Parker, O. Visser, H. S. Lichte, and S. Valentin. Simulating wireless and mobile networks in omnet++: The mixim vision. In *Proc. Int. Workshop on OMNeT++ collocated with SIMUTools*, March 2008.

[KSW⁺08]   A. Köpke, M. Swigulski, K. Wessel, D. Willkomm, P. T. K. Haneveld, T. E. V. Parker, O. W. Visser, H. S. Lichte, and S. Valentin. Simulating wireless and mobile networks in omnet++ the mixim vision. In *Proceedings of the 1st international conference on Simulation tools and techniques for communications, networks and systems & workshops*, Simutools '08, pages 71:1–71:8, ICST, Brussels, Belgium, Belgium, 2008. ICST (Institute for Computer Sciences, Social-Informatics and Telecommunications Engineering).

[KZ11]   M. Khan and Y. Zaki. Dynamic spectrum trade and game-theory based network selection in lte virtualization using uniform auctioning. In Xavier Masip-Bruin, Dominique Verchere, Vassilis Tsaoussidis, and Marcelo Yannuzzi, editors, *Wired/Wireless Internet Communications*, volume 6649 of *Lecture Notes in Computer Science*, pages 39–55. Springer Berlin / Heidelberg, 2011. 10.1007/978-3-642-21560-5_4.

[Li10]   X. Li. *Radio Access Network Dimensioning for 3G UMTS*. Vieweg+Teubner Verlag, 2010.

[LV08a]   H. S. Lichte and S. Valentin. Implementing mac protocols for cooperative relaying: a compiler-assisted approach. In *Proceedings of the 1st international conference on Simulation tools and techniques for communications, networks and systems & workshops*, Simutools '08, pages 32:1–32:10, ICST, Brussels, Belgium, Belgium, 2008. ICST (Institute for Computer Sciences, Social-Informatics and Telecommunications Engineering).

[LV08b]   H. S. Lichte and S. Valentin. Implementing mac protocols for cooperative relaying: A compiler-assisted approach. In *Proc. Int. Conf. on Simulation Tools and Techniques for Communications, Networks and Systems (SIMUTools)*, March 2008.

[LWZ⁺11]   X. Li, T. Weerawardane, Y. Zaki, C. Görg, and A. Timm-Giel. Shared transport for different radio broadband mobile technologies. In *Recent Advances* in *Broadband Integrated Network Operations and Services Management*, pages 135–159. IGI Global, June 2011.

[LZW⁺08] X. Li, Y. Zaki, T. Weerawardane, A. Timm-Giel, and C. Görg. Hsupa backhaul bandwidth dimensioning. In *Personal, Indoor and Mobile Radio Communications, 2008. PIMRC 2008. IEEE 19th International Symposium on*, pages 1 –6, sept. 2008.

[LZW⁺10] X. Li, Y. Zaki, T. Weerawardane, A. Timm-Giel, C. Görg, and G.C. Malafronte. Use of traffic separation techniques for the transport of hspa and r99 traffic in the radio access network with differentiated quality of service. In *Networking and Telecommunications: Concepts, Methodologies, Tools, and Applications*, pages 863–878. IGI Global, 2010.

[LZZ⁺12] M. Li, L. Zhao, Y. Zaki, A. Timm-Giel, and C. Görg. Investigation of network virtualization and load balancing techniques in lte networks. In *2012 IEEE 75th Vehicular Technology Conference: VTC2012-Spring*, Yokohama, Japan, May. 2012.

[Mar11] S. N. K. Marwat. Bandwidth and qos aware lte uplink scheduler. In *Master thesis*. ComNets - University of Bremen, October 2011.

[MBH⁺08] R. Mahindra, G. Bhanage, G. Hadjicristofi, I. Seskar, D. Raychaudhuri, and Y.Y. Zhang. Space versus time separation for wireless virtualization on an indoor grid. In *Proceedings of the IEEE Next Generation Internet Conference (NGI 2008)*, 2008.

[Mei12] S. Meier. congestion aware ho in lte systems. In *Diplomaarebit*. ComNets - University of Bremen, February 2012.

[Mic] Microsoft. Virtual server. http://www.microsoft.com/windowsserversystem/virtualserver/ .

[mod11] OPNET modeler. http://www.opnet.com/ , last accessed on August 2011.

[Mot] Motorola. Long term evolution (lte): A technical overview. http://www.motorola.com/web/Business/Solutions/Industry%20Solutions/Service%20Providers/Wireless%20Operators/LTE/_Document/Static%20Files/6834_MotDoc_New.pdf .

[MWZ⁺12a] S. N. K. Marwat, T. Weerawardane, Y. Zaki, C. Görg, and A. Timm-Giel. Design and performance analysis of bandwidth and qos aware lte uplink scheduler in heterogeneous traffic environment. In *8th International Wireless Communications and Mobile Computing Conference*, Limassol, Cyprus, August 2012.

[MWZ⁺12b] S. N. K. Marwat, T. Weerawardane, Y. Zaki, C. Görg, and A. Timm-Giel. Performance evaluation of bandwidth and qos aware lte uplink scheduler. In *10th International Conference on Wired/Wireless Internet Communications, WWIC 2012*, Santorini, Greece, June 2012.

[MWZ+12c]   S. N. K. Marwat, T. Weerawardane, Y. Zaki, C. Görg, and A. Timm-Giel. Performance of bandwidth and qos aware lte uplink scheduler towards delay sensitive traffic. In *17. ITG Fachtagung Mobilkommunikation*, Osnabrueck, Germany, May 2012.

[Nak09]   T. Nakamura. Proposal for candidate radio interface technologies for imt-advanced based on lte release 10 and beyond (lte-advanced). In *ITU-R WP 5D 3rd Workshop on IMT-Advanced*, October 2009.

[PDF+08]   S. Parkvall, E. Dahlman, A. Furuskar, Y. Jading, M. Olsson, S. Wanstedt, and K. Zangi. Lte-advanced - evolving lte towards imt-advanced. In *Vehicular Technology Conference, 2008. VTC 2008-Fall. IEEE 68th*, pages 1 –5, sept. 2008.

[Per09]   H. Perros. Computer simulation techniques: The definitive introduction! *http://www4.ncsu.edu/~hp//simulation.pdf* , December 2009.

[PMP+07]   A. Pokhariyal, G. Monghal, K.I. Pedersen, P.E. Mogensen, I.Z. Kovacs, C. Rosa, and T.E. Kolding. Frequency domain packet scheduling under fractional load for the utran lte downlink. In *Vehicular Technology Conference, 2007. VTC2007-Spring. IEEE 65th*, pages 699 –703, april 2007.

[PMRK06]   L. Peterson, S. Muir, T. Roscoe, and A. Klingaman. Planetlab architecture: An overview. Technical Report PDN–06–031, PlanetLab Consortium, May 2006.

[SB08]   J. Sachs and S. Baucke. Virtual radio-a framework for configurable radio networks. In *WICON'08*, Hawaii, USA, Nov. 2008.

[SBT09]   S. Sesia, M.P.J. Baker, and I. Toufik. *LTE, the UMTS long term evolution: from theory to practice*. Wiley, 2009.

[She00]   J. M. Shea. History of wireless communication. *http://wireless.ece.ufl.edu/jshea/HistoryOfWirelessCommunication.html* , December 2000.

[Sin04]   A. Singh. An introduction to virtualization. http://www.kernelthread.com/publications/virtualization/ , January 2004.

[Sta12]   StatSoft. http://www.statsoft.com/textbook/distribution-tables/ , last accessed on January 2012.

[Ste94]   W.J. Stewart. *Introduction to the numerical solution of Markov chains*. Princeton University Press, 1994.

[Ste11]   W.J. Stewart. *Probability, Markov Chains, Queues, and Simulation: The Mathematical Basis of Performance Modeling*. Princeton University Press, 2011.

[UML]   User Mode Linux UML. http://virt.kernelnewbies.org/UML .

[UZZ⁺10]   A. Udugama, L. Zhao, Y. Zaki, C. Görg, and A. Timm-Giel. End-to-end
              performance evaluation of virtual networks using prototype. In *Second In-
              ternational ICST Conference on Mobile Networks And Management (Mon-
              ami)*, Santander, Spain, September 22-24 2010.

[Val06]   S. Valentin. Chsim - a wireless channel simulator for omnet++, in tkn tu
              berlin simulation workshop.   http://www.cs.uni-paderborn.de/fileadmin/
              Informatik/AG-Karl/projects/chsim/ChSim-introduction-tkn-09-2006.pdf
              , September 2006.

[VAN]   VANU. Multiran.
              http://www.vanu.com/solutions/multiran.html .

[Vi10]   VoIP-info.org. Call quality metrics.
              http://www.voip-info.org/wiki/view/Call+Quality+Metrics , 2010.

[VMw]   VMware. http://www.vmware.com/ .

[VRO]   VROUT. http://nrg.cs.ucl.ac.uk/vrouter .

[Wee11]   T. Weerawardane. *Optimization and Performance Analysis of High Speed
              Mobile Access Network*. Vieweg & Teubner, 2011.

[WG07]   D. E. Williams and J. Garcia. Virtualization with xen: Including xenenter-
              prise, xenserver, and xenexpress. In *Syngress Publishing, Inc.*, ISBN-13:
              9781597491679, May 2007.

[WZTG⁺09]   T. Weerawardane, Y. Zaki, A. Timm-Giel, G.C. Malafronte, S. Hauth, and
              C. Görg. Impact of the transport network congestion control on the hsupa
              performance. In *Vehicular Technology Conference, 2009. VTC Spring 2009.
              IEEE 69th*, pages 1 –6, april 2009.

[Zah11]   N. Zahariev. Optimized service aware radio resource scheduler in lte. In
              Diplomaarbeit. ComNets - University of Bremen, April 2011.

[ZKZG11]   Y. Zaki, M. Khan, L. Zhao, and C. Görg. Realizing the broker based dy-
              namic spectrum allocation through lte virtualization and uniform auction-
              ing. In *Performance Evaluation of Cognitive Radio Networks. Workshop
              (PE-CRN), Networking 2011*, Valencia, Spain, May 2011.

[ZLZ⁺11]   L. Zhao, M. Li, Y. Zaki, A. Timm-Giel, and C. Görg. Lte virtualization:
              From theoretical gain to practical solution. In *Teletraffic Congress (ITC),
              2011 23rd International*, pages 71 –78, San Francisco, USA, sept. 2011.

[ZWGTG11a]   Y. Zaki, T. Weerawardane, C. Görg, and A. Timm-Giel. Long term evo-
              lution (lte) model development within opnet simulation environment. In
              OPNET workshop 2011, Washington D.C., USA, August 29-September 1
              2011.

[ZWGTG11b]   Y. Zaki, T. Weerawardane, C. Görg, and A. Timm-Giel. Multi-qos-aware
              fair scheduling for lte. In *Vehicular Technology Conference (VTC Spring),
              2011 IEEE 73rd*, pages 1 –5, may 2011.

[ZWL+08] Y. Zaki, T. Weerawardane, X. Li, A. Timm-Giel, G.C. Malafronte, and C. Görg. Effect of the rlc and tnl congestion control on the hsupa network performance. In *Communications, Computers and Applications, 2008. MIC-CCA 2008. Mosharaka International Conference on*, pages 1 –7, aug. 2008.

[ZWL+10] Y. Zaki, T. Weerawardane, X. Li, A. Timm-Giel, G.C. Malafronte, and C. Görg. Performance enhancement due to the tnl congestion control on the simultaneous deployment of both hsdpa and hsupa. In *Recent Advances in Communications and Networking Technologies, Journal of Networks*, volume 7, 2010.

[ZZGTG10a] Y. Zaki, L. Zhao, C. Görg, and A. Timm-Giel. A Novel LTE Wireless Virtualization Framework. In *Second International ICST Conference on Mobile Networks And Management (Monami).*, Santander, Spain, September 2010.

[ZZGTG10b] Y. Zaki, L. Zhao, C. Görg, and A. Timm-Giel. LTE wireless virtualization and spectrum management. In *Wireless and Mobile Networking Conference (WMNC), 2010 Third Joint IFIP*, pages 1 –6, oct. 2010.

[ZZGTG11] Y. Zaki, L. Zhao, C. Görg, and A. Timm-Giel. Lte mobile network virtualization. *Mobile Networks and Applications (MONET), ACM Journal*, pages 1–9, 2011. 10.1007/s11036-011-0321-7.

[ZZJ+09] Y. Zaki, L. Zhao, J. Jimenez, K. Mengal, A. Timm-Giel, and C. Görg. Towards interoperability among virtual networks in the future internet. In *ICT-MobileSummit 2009*, Santander Spain, June 2009.

[ZZU+11] L. Zhao, Y. Zaki, A. Udugama, U. Toseef, C. Görg, and A. Timm-Giel. Open connectivity services for future networks. In *Emerging Technologies for a Smarter World (CEWIT), 2011 8th International Conference Expo on*, pages 1–4, nov. 2011.

[ZZW+11] Y. Zaki, N. Zahariev, T. Weerawardane, C. Görg, and A. Timm-Giel. Optimized service aware lte mac scheduler: Design, implementation and performance evaluation. In *OPNET workshop 2011*, Washington D.C., USA, August 29-September 1 2011.

[ZZW+12] N. Zahariev, Y. Zaki, T. Weerawardane, X. Li, C. Görg, and A. Timm-Giel. Optimized service aware lte mac scheduler with comparison against other well known schedulers. In *10th International Conference on Wired/Wireless Internet Communications, WWIC 2012*, Santorini, Greece, June 2012.